Indus Valley Seals

NAVIGATE SUNDERBANS TIGER

Indus Valley Seals

NAVIGATE SUNDERBANS TIGER

ArputhaRani Sengupta

AGAM KALA PRAKASHAN

DELHI

First Published : 2016

ISBN : 978-81-7320-162-2

Published by:
Dr. Agam Prasad, M.A., Ph.D., Diploma in Museology
for **Agam Kala Prakashan**
34, Central Market, Ashok Vihar, Delhi-110052
Ph. : 27212195, 65688806-7 Fax : 91-11-27212195
E-mail : agambooks@gmail.com, agambook@yahoo.com
Website : www.agamkala.com

Laser Typesetting by:
Elegant Printographics
Rohini, Delhi-85.

Printed by:
Balajee Imaging Systems
Delhi - 110052

Printed in India

To my mother

Jane Jothi Sundaram

31.7.1915 – 11.9.1991

Synchronicity happens when God wishes to remain anonymous.

Message in a Bottle

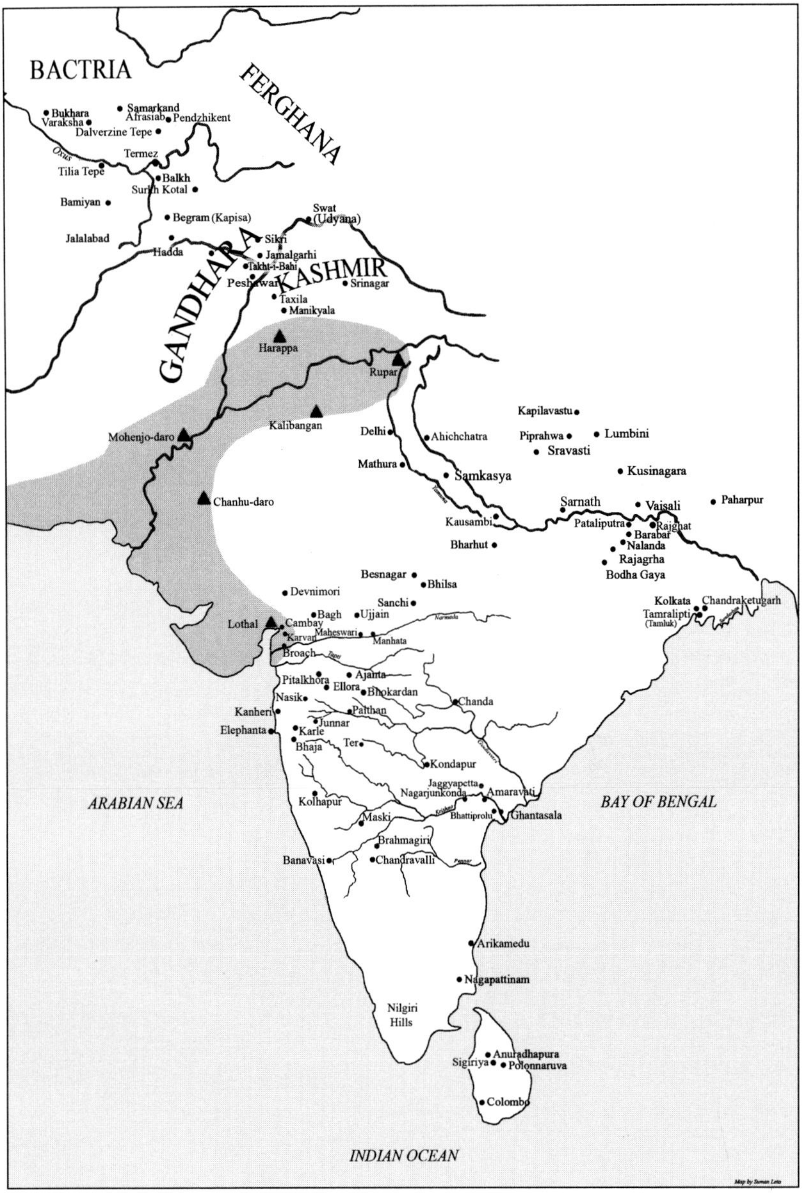

BACTRIA
FERGHANA
Bukhara
Varaksha
Samarkand
Afrasiab
Pendzhikent
Dalverzine Tepe
Oxus
Termez
Tilia Tepe
Balkh
Surkh Kotal
Bamiyan
Begram (Kapisa)
Swat (Udyana)
Jalalabad
Hadda
Sikri
Jamalgarhi
Takht-i-Bahi
GANDHARA
KASHMIR
Peshawar
Srinagar
Taxila
Manikyala
Harappa
Rupar
Kalibangan
Mohenjo-daro
Chanhu-daro
Delhi
Ahichchatra
Mathura
Samkasya
Kapilavastu
Piprahwa
Lumbini
Sravasti
Kusinagara
Sarnath
Vaisali
Paharpur
Kausambi
Pataliputra
Rajghat
Barabar
Nalanda
Rajagrha
Bodha Gaya
Bharhut
Besnagar
Bhilsa
Devnimori
Sanchi
Bagh
Ujjain
Narmada
Lothal
Cambay
Maheswari
Manhata
Karvan
Broach
Tapti
Kolkata
Chandraketugarh
Tamralipti
(Tamluk)
Pitalkhora
Ajanta
Ellora
Bhokardan
Nasik
Chanda
Kanheri
Paithan
Junnar
Elephanta
Karle
Bhaja
Ter
Kondapur
Jaggyapetta
Amaravati
Nagarjunkonda
Krishna
Bhattiprolu
Ghantasala
ARABIAN SEA
BAY OF BENGAL
Kolhapur
Maski
Brahmagiri
Banavasi
Chandravalli
Penner
Arikamedu
Nagapattinam
Nilgiri
Hills
Anuradhapura
Sigiriya
Polonnaruva
Colombo
INDIAN OCEAN

CONTENTS

PREFACE

Strange as it may seem there is a connection between the Bonabibi ballad of the Sundarbans and the tiger and goddess cult in the Indus Valley Civilization as revealed by the button seals engraved in mysterious hieroglyphs. The subject of endless speculation, the prehistoric South Asian culture is resurrected through the living tradition to ascertain their meeting point by means of the visual art of the transnational early historic period. Sundarbans, the 'Beautiful Forest' is home to ancient tiger cult dominated by goddess Bonabibi. As the name implies, Bonabibi is mistress of the forest. Bonabibi rides the tiger king worshiped as Dakshin Raya. The unique feature of the Sundarbans is the vast stretch of mangrove forests. It is a sanctuary to the ferocious tiger always referred to as the 'big cat'. The royal Bengal tiger is king of the jungle where the web of life is knitted by voracious tides, hence its pseudonym 'Tide Country'. Amitav Ghosh in his famous book *The Hungry Tide* recounts the life of the people who have chosen to live in the 24 Parganas of West Bengal where the tide and the tiger play havoc. The folk religion of the region is engaged in appeasing the tiger. The native folk seek the protection of Bonabibi and various other saints with songs and ritual worship. Bonabibi Pala is a ballad sung in praise of Bonabibi. Theatrical performance is an extension of the oral tradition and one of the modes of worship offered to the forest goddess.

The cult has generated diverse art forms. Theatrical performances accompanied by narrative songs in Bengali have played a powerful role in the production of folk epic literature and narrative scroll painting. Magic and ritual bridge the divide between the oral tradition and the folk epic. A metrical version of the folk ballad Bonabibi Pala was composed in Musalmani Bengali by Munshi Bayanaddin Saheb under the title Bonabibi Zahuranama in circa 1874. It was translated in English by Sarat Chandra Mitra in early 20th century. Folk epic literature on Bonabibi is recent compared to late medieval narrative scroll on Gazi Pir of the Sundarbans now in the British Museum. The legendary Zenda Gazi, like Bonabibi, is a Muslim saint who offers protection against all harmful animals. Gazi Pir rides a tiger called the 'Gazi's Horse'. On the whole the various cults in Sundarbans engage in compelling issues such as identity, pedagogy, ecology and conservation.

Folklore and folk religion of the 24-Parganas of West Bengal has endured clearly because the Sundarbans is the sanctuary of the royal Bengal tiger. Yet, due to ecological and climatic changes, the goddess cult linked to the living traditions based on the reverance accorded to the tiger face imminent loss in the tide country. Before we face a geographical and cultural void in the Bay of Bengal it is essential to record the astonishing magico-religious culture and commit it to memory. The story of *Riding the Tiger King* began on this note. Since remembrance also means recollection of that which is already lost it led me to recall the tree goddess and the tiger cult depicted in the Indus Valley seals.

Cult of tiger has produced unique icons of faith in the Indus Valley Culture and in the closely related Bactria Margiana Archaeological Complex (BMAC) dated to Bronze Age. Tiger is not native to these regions, but this supposedly Bronze Age cultures have produced extraordinary objects of art invoking the tiger and the goddess. On the out set cross-cultural link to the original tiger cult in the 'Gulf of the Ganges' might appear far fetched. Yet, Bay of Bengal mapped by the Elder Ptolemy is the earliest plan for the tiger hunt in antiquity that helped to disperse the tiger to much wider area. This line of investigation automatically includes other related art objects in antiquity that evidence the cult of tiger in the contemporary world. Bringing them together and viewing them in their historic context is immensely rewarding. I always found the deductive path in archaeology exciting. Deductive art history is fun. It is like solving a puzzle or connecting the evidences in a deductive episode. Take for instance the dating of prehistoric sites in the Indus Valley. To the budding archaeologist in the early twentieth century surface find of flint scrapers has been a decisive factor to judge any ancient archaeological site as prehistoric Bronze Age in South Asia (3000-1900 BC). Indus Valley culture has yielded sophisticated copper and iron implements along with exotic objects in silver and electrum. No one seems to have considered flint scrapers as ritual votive deposits in what appears to be clusters of interconnected necropolis including BMAC. The mortuary monument called the Great Stupa dominating Mohenjodaro belongs to early historic Indo-Greek Kushana period synchronal to the Roman Empire. Archaeologist K. N. Dikshit following the footsteps of M. S. Vats and Sir John Marshal was baffled by the fact that certain Kushana sites actually co-exist with the prehistoric level identified by flint scrapers.

Setting aside the ambiguous flint let us follow the tiger trail in the Sundarbans. It takes us on our first sea voyage from the Bay of Bengal to the Indus Valley. As the tiger cult spread wide, the quest for the tiger actually begins in the Mediterranean Basin. Tiger cult spread worldwide in antiquity when the tiger was first transformed into the divine transport of deities. The phenomenon of the New Age is displayed simultaneously in the sacred mosaic pavements in the Mediterranean North Africa, Asia, Europe and Roman Britain. Tiger cult in the context of transnational adoration of Bacchus supposedly born in India was possibly triggered by belief in afterlife. There seems to be no feasible explanation for the fledgling cult to spread to lands thousands of kilometers apart. From Loulan desert burials tigers leap in a fragment of golden brown Han silk (Stein no. L.C.ii.01). A piece of yellow silk with overall pattern of brown tiger stripes come from the same collection at the National Museum of India (Stein no. L.C.ix.02).

Tiger skin and natural silk convey metamorphosis of the soul. In Chinese belief when the spirit of the tiger entered the earth it transformed into golden amber, which is another sign of immortality. The purpose of this comparative study is to find the relevance of the tiger cult in the pan-cultural context.

The tiger cult stradles the desire for the preservation of one's life forever. Successful tiger hunt was due to the safe and swift travel across land and sea that reached unprecedented height in the Roman world. Pax Romana was the most important factor in the capture and transportation of the royal Bengal tiger into the Indus Valley, Roman Britain and countries along the Mediterranean, including the Greek colony in Southern Italy. With comparative visual evidence I set out to demonstrate the actual process of the wide dispersion of tigers. During the Roman period Bactria Margiana and Indus Valley were under Greco-Tocharians having affinity with the Celts. Group of Celts consecrating a stupa in mid first century AD are recorded in a relief in the Sanchi stupa in Central India. At this time Greco-Buddhist reliquary cult ushered a literate society that adapted from Aramaic linear Brahmi and cursive Kharoshti. Sir Alexander Cunningham (DG, ASI. 1861-1885) noticed a connection between the Indus script and Brahmi. From the technical point of view the specialized sample of Indus hieroglyphs engraved on the steatite seals and the recently discovered Kabul MS in birch bark written in Indus hieroglyphs follows the pattern of diffusion in present day Turkmenistan, Afghanistan and Pakistan. The (re)discovery of a long "lost" civilization and its mysterious script is possibly at hand with the discovery of Kabul manuscript in Indus script. Since birch bark MS is typical of Tocharian-Kushana period, the morphology of tiger cult evidenced by inscribed Indus seals might help actual recovery of the Indus Valley civilization about which no historical information exists.

In gladiatorial combats tiger was just one of the uncommon exotic animals. However, popularity of the tiger in worldwide Roman religion had greater impact on the commissioned tiger hunts. Trappers went forth accompanied by a well knit guild of artists. Connected with this group were traders and transporters linked across an extensive road and sea network connecting the various cult centers. It is remarkable that in the regions where the tiger is not present the tiger is represented in a most realistic and lively manner. Surprisingly the hub of the network was Central Asia and the tiger from the Bay of Bengal traveled through its arteries spread deep into Mohenjodaro and Gonur, the type site of BMAC. The jeweled tiger from Gonur is similar to the plump tiger that gazes up at the tree goddess in the Indus Valley seals. In a rare Indus seal tree goddess and tiger merge together and transform into theriomorphic tiger goddess.

In the extraordinary cultural scenario of the Indus Valley, organized community of workers rose to the maximum level of performance to produce extraordinary inscribed seals. Cultural Intelligence or cultural quotient (CQ) is best demonstrated by the individual interactions across cultures. The exquisitively carved and glazed intaglio seals in steatite demonstrate exceptional quality understood as the capability to relate and work effectively with its necromantic function. At the most obvious level, Indus culture consists of unique artifacts in which engraved seals are inscribed in cryptographs. Egyptian hieroglyphics is example of earliest cryptography. Geometric precision, realistic engraving of animals and cryptography of the gem like seals is the proof of technology transfer and development of cross cultural ideas, connections, and interdependencies.

The seed is the culturally cohesive Buddhist art and architecture through which confident and erudite innovators took the time to implement their cross-cultural competency in order to produce a booming reliquary cult in the extreme Orient. Early historic artifacts in India are referred to as Indo-Greek and the predominant language system Indo-European. Not with standing, few would acknowledge this on the assumption that Indian culture is geographically circumscribed unique product. It is unique in the sense Indian culture miraculously shares its core values regardless of religious syneretism and despite multicultural, multi racial and multi lingual plurality. It begins with the Pythagoreans. Beyond the then known world, parallel to the Age of the Buddha is the international Brotherhood at the School of Semicircle founded by Pythagoras in the ancient city of Croton. Consider the response of Pythagoras (c. 570-495 BC) when exposed to the knowledge systems in Egyptian, Babylonian, Syrian and Greek cultures. The shared ideas on philosophy, symbolism, astrology and rebirth supported by iconography and combined with the art of mathematics and geometry created worldwide productive working relationships and unprecedented globalisation in South Asia. At the birth of the New Age, the first step of the Greco-Buddhist Brotherhood was getting to know the partner culture and to build the applied knowledge as a collective whole. These are the conditions that India has taken in its stride to take advantage of in the global culture today. In the fertile grounds of the New Elysium what began as encrypted stone tablets of the Indus Valley seals are today elegant mathematical questions solved in multicultural settings by those like Manjul Bhargava (Fields Medal Prize 2014) and Subhash Khot (Nevanlinna Prize 2014).

Kolkata
15 August 2015

ArputhaRani Sengupta

I

Indus Valley Seal –Roman Mosaic

> Nowhere on Earth does humanity present itself in such a dizzying, creative burst of cultures, religions, races and tongues… It is this variety which provides a breathtaking ensemble for experiences that is uniquely Indian.
>
> Romain Rolland. *A Rough Guide to India.*

The most important factor affecting tiger hunt was the immense geographic extent of the Roman world. First, the capture of Egypt and the North African provinces of Mauretania and Numidia enlarged sources for the variety of wild animals for Rome. Pliny mentions Numidian bears pitted against Ethiopian hunters in a game held in 61 BC (NH.8.54.131). In other references, King Bocchus of Mauretania sent native spearmen to take part in the games given by Sulla in 93 BC. They were apparently expert hunters, whose skill was very likely used by Romans for the capture of wild beasts. Steady demand of exotic animals for entertainment and gladiatorial show extended into regions beyond the Roman Empire. According to Strabo, following the Roman annexation of Egypt there was an increase in Roman contact with India. By the time of Augustus up to 120 ships were setting sail every year from Myos Hormos to India[1]. Greek knowledge of the East in the first century ended at India and Ceylon. By next century the Alexandrian geographer Ptolemy (90-168AD) surprisingly spotted almost accurate number of 22,000 islands in the Indian Ocean, which he called "the Leek-Green Sea" (Prasodes Thalassa). He knew of the Golden Khersonese (Sumatra) and the Isle of Silver and placed the mysterious cities of Cattigara and Thina (China) on the eastern rim of the world.

WILD ANIMAL EXPERTS:
Capture / Transport / Care in antiquity

Cicero who died in 43 BC mentions a group of hunters known as "the shikarees" who were called upon to capture large felines such as panthers or leopards in Laodicea (Fam. 2.11.2). The words Shikar (Hunt) and Shikaree (Hunter) were readily absorbed into the local languages in the north and northwestern regions of the Indian subcontinent. The single unifying factor is the monsoon. From the Roman times people sailing the monsoon winds, southwest in summer and from the northeast in the winter, have crisscrossed heavy traffic across the Indian Ocean for trade that included silk, spice and exotic animals. The animals from Africa and Asia survive in Roman art, most notably in the hunting mosaics from North Africa, Turkey and Piazza Armerina in Sicily in southern Italy. Hunting was in general an élite activity. Throughout the imperial period, hunts (venations) were sponsored by emperors and wealthy citizens. Hunting itself was exclusive, hunters and trappers were presumably members of hereditary clans. In Roman visual culture hunts are more common than gladiatorial combats with wild beasts. Roman mosaics usually represent nobles and their attendants engaged in the hunt (1.1). Roman soldiers hardly participate in hunting expeditions. Hundreds and thousands of animals exhibited by Romans include tigers, lions, leopards, elephants, bulls, hyenas, rhinoceroses, apes, crocodiles, gazelles, and ostriches, among others. It is recorded that Julius Caesar's triumphal parade displayed elephants, lions, bulls, and a giraffe (NH.8.53; D.C. 43.23; Suet. Jul.39.3).[2]

1.1 Tiger Hunt, Roman Mosaic, 5th century AD
Great Palace of Constantinople, Turkey

Recently the big cats of Ali, a businessman in Lahore, were in the news. Ali owns six Bengal tigers reportedly imported from Canada. Ali's tigers, particularly a rare white tiger named Sandra, were a frequent feature at Nawaz Sharif's rallies in Pakistan. The popular name for Sharif is 'Sher', an Urdu word applicable equally to tiger and lion. More importantly, the exotic tiger, admired for its regal bearing and virility, is the party symbol of Sharif's Pakistan Muslim League-Nawaz (PML-N). In March 2012 one of Ali's tigers stood on a car during Sharif's campaign in Lahore, Pakistan's second-largest city — to attract attention and bring victory and power through the actual roaring tiger logo.

Magical belief in the tiger is quite ancient in the Indus Valley region. Lahore, located close to Kalibangan, a peculiar Indus culture site in Rajasthan, is recorded by Ptolemy. The 2nd century Egyptian astronomer and geographer's *Geographia* contains all that was known about the world's geography in the Roman Empire. Ptolemy locates Labokla (Lahore) on the route between the Indus River and Palibothra or Pataliputra (Patna) crossing a country called Kasperia (Kashmir). Lahore was described as extending along the rivers Bidastes or Vitasta (Jhelum), Sandabal or Chandra Bhaga (Chenab), and Adris or Iravati (Ravi). Taxila, a major Buddhist reliquary site, is on River Jhelum. In early Buddhist art the usual support for the throne is lion. However, tiger claw amulet and tiger pelt apron or seat were popular fetish in sympathetic magic. It is based on the idea that power of one thing passes on to another simply because they look similar, or that one thing is the cause of another.

Introduced by Japanese brand, modern Zoo Jeans is custom made 'Power' denim with tiger ripping. It is typical of primitive thought. In the Indus seals the tiger merges with the goddess. If we go by the votive seals, goddess and tiger together were the focus of a mystery cult prototypical of current cults. The cultural implication of the living tradition of the goddess-tiger cult in the Bay of Bengal is reserved for the second part of this discussion. First it is about how the Royal Bengal Tiger from the Sundarbans rode into the Indus Valley. And the practical consideration of how to capture and transport a ferocious tiger all that way to the Colosseum in Rome. Information is gathered primarily from Roman art and textual sources. The mixed methods used in animal capture are found in the descriptive details of Roman mosaics. Elder Pliny regrets that the lion captured in pit trap was a rather mean method against a noble animal (NH. 8.21.54). Baiting by stealing the tiger cubs was a dependable tactics for capturing the tigress (NH. 8.25.66).[3] This deceitful technique is still the staple of Theravada Buddhist monks at their tiger conservation centre in Thailand. Following the worldwide broadcast of a two-part television documentary by Animal Planet on the Thai Tiger Temple in Kanchanaburi, tiger tourism increased by an average of 900 international visitors each day. Founded in 1994 as a forest temple and sanctuary for wild tigers, it is one of the few places in the world where one can stroll with the tiger and pet or even pose with the ferocious feline for a memorable photo. According to a disgruntled volunteer, on the other hand, behind the façade of tiger mysticism at the Tiger Temple is cruelty to the tigress and trafficking in tiger cubs[4] This is the exact scenario captured by Piazza Armerina Mosaic in Sicily.

STAGE FOR WORLDWIDE ANIMISM: Cultural / Historical / Archaeological evidence

Indications are that there were tiger sanctuaries dedicated to the Mysteries of the Divine Female, Orpheus and Dionysus in the ancient Mediterranean countries and South Asia. Roman mosaic depicting the tiger in a villa at Lod in Israel is dedicated to Dionysus. Carthaginians and their Sicilian-Greek allies celebrated the Mystery cult in luxurious country houses. One of them is Piazza Armerina del Casale popularly called Piazza Armerina in Sicily. The Roman villa of great grandeur contains the richest, largest and most complex collection of Roman mosaics in the world. Remarkably, Venus and cupid at the Roman villa have a dot on the forehead. This religious mark unique to Hindu India is also found on the first century Venus in Buddhist Gandhara. Embossed in gold, the Venus plaques were recovered from Taxila and Tillya Tepe (1.2).

We tend to remember through the documented. The rest, even if real, becomes an abstraction. Piazza Armerina surrounded by a huge estate and similar to the Thai Tiger Temple, might have served as conservatory and breeding centre for tigers used in rituals. The Great Hunt mosaic at Piazza Armerina includes a captive tigress pensively gazing at her cub (1.4). At the background is a cabin with bars very much like a zoo cage. Located about 3 km outside the town of Piazza Armerina in southern Italy, its archaeology in the late 19th century coincides with the Age of Discovery in South Asia. The mosaic pavement of an apsidal shrine depicts Isis-Venus holding crescent moon. The goddess surrounded by tiger cubs in a forest is worshiped by a tigress and an elephant (1.5).

Similar to the Adoration of Venus, the iconography of goddess Lakshmi appeared earliest in the first century Greco-Buddhist art. Coincidently churned out of the ocean, Gajalakshmi as the elixir life is lustrated by paired elephants. In the vast expanse of Piazza Armerina mosaic, 'The Kiss' depicts Venus and Adonis in embrace. The circular composition at the centre is surrounded by portrait heads of 'Star cult members' separated by Celtic interlacement. The 'endless knot' is a Buddhist symbol denoting 'Endless Time' or eternity. The image of Sacred Marriage is an exceptional witness to the Greco-Buddhist reliquary cult in Gandhara, where 'The Kiss' is replicated in an engraved Roman blue glass (1.3). Along with this the classical Parinirvana and the rebirth of the Buddha indicates that the ressurected lord took many forms in the Roman world in search for immortality.

1.2 Venus, Gold, 5 x 2.6 cm, Tillya Tepe Tomb VI Ist century AD, Kabul : National Museum

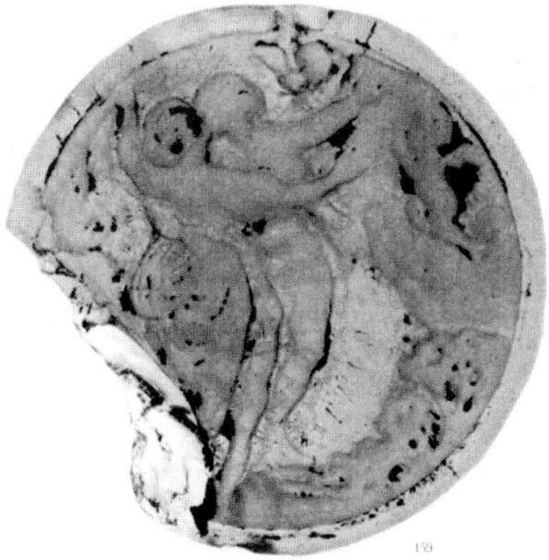

1.3 Venus and Adonis, Roman Glass, Gandhara, 1st century AD Collection A.I.C.

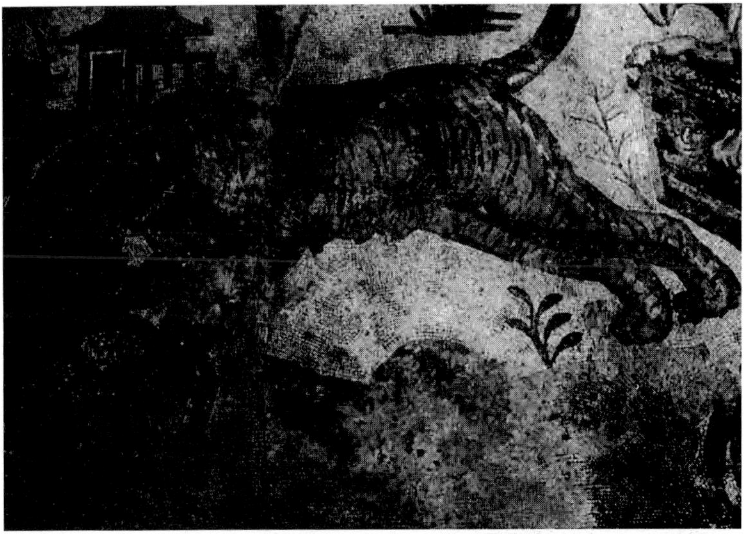

1.4 Tigress with cub, Roman mosaic, Piazza Armerina, Sicily, Italy

1.5 Adoration of Isis-Venus, Roman mosaic, Piazza Armerina, Sicily, Italy

Alexandrian navigators on fast ships riding the monsoon winds rapidly transported variety of consignments across the seas. Along with the luxury goods, commercial exploitation of exotic animals from India is predictable. The Indian Ocean trading networks linked with Mediterranean Africa and Europe had both maritime and overland contact with Syria, Parthia and India. Rapid transit of animals from North Africa to Ostia, the port of Rome, sailed in just two days, perhaps propelled also by oars (NH. 19.4). In comparison to Asian elephants ideal for display the mamoth Africa elephants were prized for ivory from ancient time. The Elder Pliny regrets that in addition to camouflaged pit-traps (NH. 8.8.24) the elephants were ambushed and captured (NH. 8.5.9). Juba, king of Mauretania (25 BC – circa 23 AD) observed that hunters dug pits to capture elephants (Plu. Mor.972b). Netting and chaining them for transport was customary. Dignity and nobility of the elephant, like that of its size and gait, was

1.6 Caesar Elephant, Silver Denarius, Rome, 49 BC.

1.7 Elephant seal, Steatite, Mohenjo-Daro, Proto-historic period

1.8 Elephant head, Terracotta, Mohenjo-Daro, Proto-historic period

admired for its association with Saturn, the majestic planet Maha Kala. The elephant's awesome power demonstrated in the Punic Wars (264-146 BC) combined with Roman mythology of Saturn as the King of the Golden age made Julius identify himself as Caesar the elephant. Caesar in Punic meant elephant. As the victor of Gallia (Spain) and Britain, Caesar on a Republican Roman coin was personified as an elephant trampling the Celtic carnyx (1.6). The elephant synonymous to a glorious king transformed the Imperial Cult of Rome in the entire known world.

The religious belief in elephant's nature is skillfully conveyed in early Indian art. The domesticated Asian elephants depicted in Greco-Buddhist art are far removed from the wild. The elephant on the Mohenjo-Daro seals are depicted with the same human considerations (1.7). Inexplicably, ivory tusks recovered from Taxila and Mohenjodaro nearby were that of

1.9 Pashupati seal, Steatite seal, 3.56 x 3.53 cm, thickness 0.76 cm. Mohenjo-Daro, Proto-historic period, (Mackay 1928)

African elephant. An unusual elephant seal from the Oxus trading network is inscribed in the Indus script. It is one among several artifacts recovered from Bactria-Margiana Archaeological Complex that serve as a building block in animal mysticism (3.5). What is unexpected is to come across Alexandrian style in Mohenjo-Daro known as the Mound of the Dead in the Sind province of Pakistan (1.8). A realistic elephant head in faience from Hellenized Egypt has the same modulation of form seen in the Indus Valley terracotta fragment presumed to be from Bronze Age.[5] Elephant appears alongside the tiger in a rare seal in which a Buddha like seated deity with antlers is surrounded by iconic animal species; tiger and elephant to right and rhino and buffalo left (1.9). While directing excavations in Mohenjo-Daro (1928-29) E.J.H. Mackay discovered this unusual seal in Block 1, Southern Portion of the DK-G Area. He numbered the seal 420 and named it "Pashupati" and dated it to the Intermediate I Period (2600–1900 BC) in his 1937-38 report.

1.10 Osho-Pashupati, Gold stater, Kanishka I, c. 78-115 AD
1.11 Offering Tray, Schist, D. 15.4 cm, Ist century AD, Metropolitan Museum of Art, New York : (1987.142.41)

In the crossroads of cultures the 'Pashupati' seal seem to derive from various sources. It's similarity with the "Cernunnos" type of antlered Celtic god on the Gundestrup Cauldron has been widely commented upon. The cauldron discovered in Denmark is stylistically similar to Thracian silver work probably made between 150 BC and the birth of Christ. Pair of long-horned gazelle depicted beneath the low seat of Pashupati is like a cryptic label. The gazelle, from Arabic Ghazal meaning 'elegant and quick' is archaic metaphor for female beauty. From other Indus seals we can identify the crested deity as divine female. The three-headed deity crowned like cow goddess Hathor is decked with rows of necklaces and bangles. She wears girdled tunic with long sleeves with crinkles covering her arms. The sleeve of Kushana king Kanishka II is treated in similar manner on one of his gold Osho-Pashupati coins. The Egyptian concept of divine king as the "Bull in Heaven" begins with Kanishka I (circa 78-115 AD). Inscribed in Tocharian Middle Iranian Aryan language, "Osho" the three headed deity with four arms stands against a bull (1.10).

1.12 Tiger goddess seal, Steatite, Mohenjo-Daro, Indus Valley
1.13 Tiger goddess, Cylinder seal, Faience, Kalibangan, Rajasthan
1.14 Resurrection Vignette, Book of the Dead, New Kingdom, Egypt

The story of hunters and animal collectors is inexplicably connected to Greco-Buddhist reliquary cult. While hunters targeted animal reserves, geomancers undertook the arcane task of locating reliquary stupa sites and supplementary rock cut monuments in remote pristine hills surrounded by springs and forests. Intuitively they located singular energy centers conducive for regeneration. But they had to roam over great distances and cross streams and rivers to reach inaccessible regions in Gandhara, Indus Valley and the rocky sites on east and west coast of India. Along with hunters and geomancers experienced tomb makers arrived from Egypt, Turkey and Palmyra. It resulted in the proliferation of rock-cut caves in the Indian subcontinent. Among the early monuments elephants carved out of living rock at Dauli and Udayagiri are remarkable. The early historic

Hathigumpha and Tiger caves in Odisha on the west coast, like several others, incorporate animal symbolism.

The sphinx as guardian of the tomb in Greek and Egyptian art is peculiar to both Buddhist and Indus Valley cultures. The so called 'Toilet Tray' of Taxila are actually offering plates dedicated to the departed in stupa shrines on the banks of Jhelum. The soul saucers carved in schist are substitute for the Indus seals. Similar to the Roman pavement mosaics Isis-Venus offers salvation and as mistress of the sea rides aquatic dragon, hippocampus and leogryph on the offering tray (1.11). In the Indus Valley seal the morphed goddess merges with the tiger (1.12). The divine female identified with various animals seems to answer the question: Who will offer solemn supplications at death? By whom will divine sacrifices be made? In the early historic period these questions were central to the reliquary cult. From Kalibangan a curious cylindrical seal fashioned in faience reveals that the tiger goddess administered resurrection of the dead (1.13). The vignette is comparable to the lustration scene in the "Book of the Dead" from New Kingdom Egypt. The painting illustrates incarnation of the double (Ka) of the departed (1.14).

RIDING THE TIGER: Religious / Magical accounts

Tigers occupy a variety of habitats — tropical evergreen forests, deciduous shrub and thorn jungles and mangrove swamps. Distribution of tiger in India is practically throughout the country, from the Himalayas to the Cape Comorin, except in Punjab, Kutch and the deserts of Rajasthan. Pakistan and Afghanistan in the northwest did not have tiger. The tiger in the multi-cultural Indus Valley civilization, like its dating, is an anachronism. Periyar Tiger Reserve at Thekkady in Kerala might have played an

1.15 Bacchus Mosaic, D.114 cm, Roman Britain, 1st-2nd century AD, London: The British Museum (AO 290)

important role in the export tiger and import of tiger lore.[6] Infant Ayyappa, according to the popular belief, was found on the Pampa River. His foster mother who wished the child dead sent him to bring tiger milk to cure her headache. Miraculously, Ayyappa rode back on a tigress heavy with milk.[7] Iconography of Lord Ayyappa riding a tigeress is similar to the Carthaginian Dionysus believed to be born in India or having visited India. Muzuris on the west-coast in contact with Phoenicians, Egyptians and

Greeks was vital to the trade and cultural exchange between south India and the Roman Empire.

Iinfant Dionysus worshiped in Carthage triumphantly rides a tigress engorged with milk in a first century Roman mosaic at Tunisia. The fertility god wears leopard-skin and holds thyrsos staff. Typically the 'Triumph of Bacchus' represents Dionysus on a chariot pulled by tigers as in the second century mosaics at the Archaeological Museum at Sousse and Madrid. Dionysus in a Roman mosaic in situ at El Djem wears leopard-skin and holds a thyrsos staff (Cat. no. TBA). The tiger that gained centre stage in the neo-Dionysian cult spread from Ethiopia and North Africa to Asia and Europe.[8] The Leadenhall Street Mosaic of Bacchus riding a tiger is earlier than most surviving mosaics from Roman Britain (1.15). It was discovered in 1803 during building work on the premises of the East India Company in London. The myth that Bacchus visited India is indicated by the tiger rather than the more usual spotted leopard. In a North African Roman mosaic the popular subject of the 'Triumph of Bacchus in India' indicates the return of the 'dying god', as if from some place beyond the borders of the known world. In the 'Wrath of Dionysus' the pirates of Tyrrhenian Sea, all except Acoetes the helmsman, were changed to dolphins by Dionysus. Alluding to her arrival from the sea and as a sign of metamorphosis, the goddess in Buddhist art stands on dolphin-makara pedestal. In the Bacchanal scenes in Greco-Buddhist art, the god of the harvest, grapes and wine accompanied by Ariadne celebrates ritual madness, ecstasy and drinking (1.16). Works of art indicate that Bacchus along with the divine female was worshipped in India as early as first century. In the regrettably defaced 'Drunken Bacchus' a Greco-Syrian woman plies a rotund man with wine (1.17). Representations of drinking and wide variety of wine vessels in early Buddhist art suggest that the cult was popular across Gandhara and north India. Unusual stone moulds for the two halves of a wine cup from Kausmabi are carved with Bacchanal scenes. Pair of revelers wear bird mask on one side; harpist accompanies dancing female in flowing Greek chiton on the other half of the mold (1.18). Realistic description of the scene inclined towards portraiture is also the most significant development in Roman mosaics and murals. At the circular bottom of the mold is a band of vine tendrils with lotus of rebirth at the centre.

In the cusp of sea change era, animals that were normally viewed as commodities, traded and exploited for entertainment and profit, became treasured religious symbols. Significantly, representation of animal combat in gladiatorial events is much less compared to their appearance in hunting scenes juxtaposed with religious images. Mysteries of Dionysus and Orpheus that used animal symbolism extensively as sign of rebirth and heavenly bliss gained wide following.[9] Orphism was said to have invented the Mysteries of Dionysus. Priest of Dionysus called Dionysia officiated Feasts of Eleusis and Ceres. Significantly, Christianity, which in its earliest days shared a good deal with many "mystery religions", was declared the state religion of Rome in 313. It introduced new kind of religious art still connected to ancient myths and religion. Orpheus, the enchanting musician and legendary prophet in Greek religion and myth, was identified with Christ Entranced animals occupying Orphic mosaics are found in several late Roman villas. The tiger is in a ring of beasts separated by trees with sometimes an intermediate ring of birds that includes peacock denoting rebirth. At the centre of this circular composition is resurrected Orpheus. The whole is then framed in a square

1.16 Pillar of Immortality, Sandstone, Mathura, H. 80 cm, 2nd century AD, Ohio: Cleveland Museum of Art (77.34) John S. Severan Fund

1.17 Drunken Bacchus, Mathura, 2nd century AD, Kolkata: Indian Museum (N.S.4192)

1.18 Wine goblet, Stone mold, 6 x 7 cm, Kausambi, 2nd century AD, Allahabad University Museum

1.19 'The Orpheus' Roman mosaic, Cirencester Corinium Museum

with complex geometric patterns.[10] We note that the tiger striding majestically in the Orpheus Mosaic at the Cirencester Corinium Museum is typical of Roman realism (1.19). Likewise, the naturalistic tiger engraved in an Indus seal fragment holds a mirror to nature. Considering the small scale and the reverse process of intaglio, it required outstanding skill and personal experience of the animal (1.20). The seals in particular reveal new geographies and thoughts that may or may not resemble the referenced-real site. In an inscribed seal the tiger is detached from its natural disposition and placed in front of an 'offering tray' as a sign of apotheosis (1.21). It is composed in the manner of religious scenes in which the 'pet' tiger or leopard is a scared sign in Dionysian mosaics. The offering tray and the tiger as an embodiment of a royal person would have had significant role in funerary cult rituals. It is in this context that the un-deciphered script would have conveyed its message. The seals, like the rest of planning, show

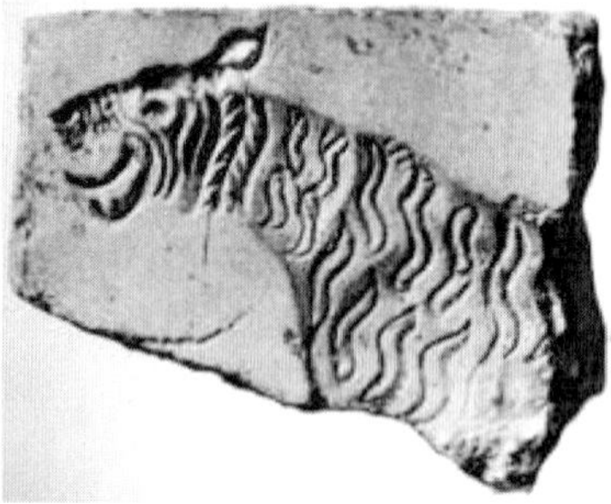

1.20 Tiger seal, Steatite, Mohenjo-Daro, Proto-historic period

1.21 Tiger offering tray, Steatite seal, Mohenjo-Daro

astonishing level of preparation, organization and execution to serve a particular function. Significantly, the pictographs engraved on seals show no signs of having passed through a formative phase. Further, the long tradition essential to gem engraving is absent in the secluded Indus Valley. The homogeneity and the quantity of seals seem to indicate that the ephemeral seals depended on imported technology — Egypt comes first as author of the votive tablets. Evidence indicates that the seals were made within a short period of less than one hundred years. Suddenly appearing and disappearing, the Indus reliquary cult is as short lived as the Greco-Buddhist reliquary cult spread across the Indus

Valley and the subcontinent. The Great Kushana Stupa crowning the manmade citadel at Mhenjo-Daro in fact helps us to uphold this perspective.

RELATIONAL MEMORY: Swastika / Triskelon / Wheel

The most common type of anachronism is an object misplaced in time. Misled by the 20th century archaeology, we cannot experience Harappan culture at the summit of events. Pockets of abandoned cult sites, including isolated Mohenjo-Daro, were discovered in the 1920s. Disjointed by the undeciphered seals, Harappa and Mohenjo-Daro coexist with the Greco-Buddhist reliquary cult in the Indus Valley that flourished during the early centuries of the Christian era. In spite of escalation of human activities, Harappa sites were apparently untouched by the unprecedented influx of Greco-Romans. When items peculiar to Buddhist cult, such as the Great Stupa in Mohenjo-Daro, come to our notice in the Harappan sites, they are studiously ignored rather than acknowledged. Both Harappan and Buddhist sites are mystifying precisely because of the exotic material culture of the mystery cults. Decline of the Roman Empire signaled abrupt desertion of Buddhist and Indus sites. In the binery process the past was entirely discarded and replaced by a civilization built on extraordinary synthesis. Now, the essential question is how do we remember, through reliving experiences or documentation? Memories ingrained in the exceptional manmade objects suggests other ways to approach them. Morphology is one way through which we may recollect the past.

The easiest is to consider the dialectics of material and the method of communication. A button seal in pale

1.22 Swastika seal, Faience, H.0.7 cm, Mohenjo-Daro (DK 10049), London : The British Museum (OA 1947.4-16.8) Presented by Govt. of India 1947

1.23 Swastila offering tray, Schist, D.11.25 cm, Sirkap, Taxila Ist century AD, Pakistan: Taxila Museum (193-1932-33)

yellow-green faience is engraved with swastika (1.22). Faience is fossil type in Egypt while swastika associated with the Greek was widespread in Mediterranean cultures. From the time of Philip II of Macedon and his son Alexander the Great, the Celt associates of the Greek kingdom considered swastika sacred. Experienced in mining silver and minting coins, the Celts were capable of producing thousands of coins that show just a few milligrams each side of the intended weight. They could also make subtle alterations to the quality of the alloy, masking a decrease in the precious metal content. These are the admirable quality of the earliest silver punch-mark coins in South Asia. Like the seals, hoards of ritually buried punch-mark coins are surrounded by considerable degree of mystery and unsatisfactory explanations about their origin and use. Among these cast copper votives with railed swastika standard on reverse and elephant on obverse is peculiar relic of Sri Lanka. This ancient Buddhist token from Anuradhapura and Jaffna was reported first by

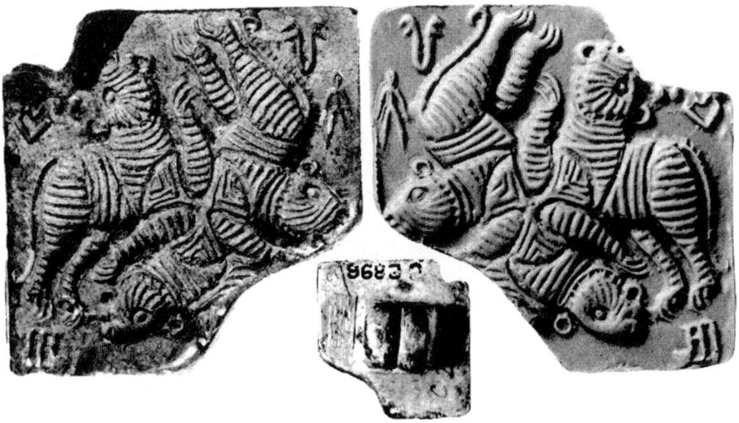

1.24 Triskelon tiger, Mohenjo-Daro (M-295) (Parpola and Joshi, vol.I)

Codrington. The closest votive offering is swastika Soul Saucer from Taxila, which like the other offering trays, is certainly connected to the eastern Mediterranean (1.23).

The Indus Valley steatite seals were mainly surface finds deposited at gateways and cult chambers. But more can be learned from the artistic compositions themselves. Let us consider an unusual square seal in which three striped tigers share their foreleg. Without disregarding the possibility of animal personification, the tigers rotate around a trifoil axis (1.24). The peculiar Celtic triple sign called Triskelon is integrated in several ways in Mohenjo-Daro. Artifacts having trefoil pattern simulating leopard skin range from resist dyed faience bead to trilobite design on the off-shoulder costume of the bearded priest (1.25). A deer offering plate excavated at Barikot in Paksitan alters the traditional Welsh Celtic Triskelt called the 'Triple Horse Circle' into 'Triple Deer Circle'. In the Triskelon offering tray the animals share three ears yet each appears to have two (1.26). Interpretive Celtic triple sign was not confined to Gandhara, where the Barikot votive terracotta

1.25 Bearded Priest KIng, Mohenjo-daro
1.26 Triskelon deer, Terracotta, Barikot, Swat: Saidu Sharif Museum, Pakistan
1.27 Triskelon, engraving in a cave at Junnar, Mahrashtra (Begley)

served important function in the Greco-Buddhist reliquary cult. Begley reported Triskelon engraving in an isolated cave in Junnar discovered among some 252 rock-cut caves scattered in the Western Ghats where leopards roam even now (1.27). The tessellated Triskelon pattern was originally a Roman method used in pavements. The Junnar engraving is prototypical of modern pavements that use precast interlocking blocks.

According to an inscription in Junnar cave complex, Satavahana king Satakarni proclaims Vedishri at its very center. Vedishri might denote goddess Shri Devi as source of knowledge. The inscription describes Satakarni as the "Lord of Dakshinapatha, wielder of the unrestrained wheel of sovereignty". In *De Bello Gallica* Julius Caesar refers to Celtic god Taran as "he who held the empire of the skies". The so-called Celtic 'wheel god' Taranis or Taran is literally thunder. Taranis as Jupiter is the Roman wheel of triumph that identified a noble person as divine. The wheel represents the elemental force of nature associated with the sky. In all likelihood the 'thunder wheel' could just as easily be a 'solar wheel'. The wheel called Srichakra of

1.28 Bull seal, Steatite, Mohenjo-Daro, Proto-historic period, Karachi: National museum
1.29 Rhinoceros, Steatite, Indus Valley Seal

Lakshmi is attribute of Isis-Nemesis. The goddess of retribution was widely represented as winged griffin in Greco-Buddhist art.

Buddhist reliquary cult shares cultural affinity with Greco-Roman cults of the period. The solar halo and the chariot drawn by four horses came to be identified as sign of glorification of immortals. The Wheel of Law turned by Hellenistic Buddha too is associated with eternal life and immense radiance. The wheel is an important sign in the hieroglyphic inscription that offers in the Indus Valley seal the magnificent humped bull as the choicest sacrifice. It describes the 'Triumphant' Soul riding the wheel of fortune for all eternity (1.28). In the pictographic system the wheel always takes the lead, whether seen from the right or from the left (1.29). The erudite artist dedicated to communicate the divine employs his skill in an impeccable manner. Steeped in symbolism, the exotic rhinoceros depicted true to life is comparable to Egyptian oeuvre in animal representation.

The inscribed seals are token of victory over death. The seals carved in dull steatite have no reflective power but when low fired gains self luminosity. The hieroglyphics

1.30a. Celts consecrating Greco-Buddhist stupa, North Gateway, Sanchi Stupa I, 1st century AD
1.30b. Musicians playing Celtic carnyces or aulos, Detail of relief, Sanchi Stupa I, Ist century AD

in the Triskelt Tiger seal are scattered in the field. Inscription in a horizontal register at the top is the customary. To the Egyptians inscribed words "swifter than greyhounds and quicker than light" performed powerful magic. The Indus Valley pictograms animate the inanimate. The sequences and patterns in the script clearly convey code in the form a cipher underlying logic of a verbal communication system. However, the language remains a mystery since the cryptic code was invented for esoteric purpose. The as yet un-deciphered pictographic Indus script bears certain resemblance to Egyptian hieroglyphics and Celtic runes. Rune means mystery or secret in early English and related languages. Both Egyptian and Celtic skill in the occult was valued in ancient time. On the north gateway of Sanchi stupa datable to about mid first century, we come across a group of Celtic Druid, bards and musicians consecrating a Buddhist stupa (1.30a). Their ethnic identity is confirmed by carnyce blowers to left (1.30b). Winged bird as adoring human spirit hovers above the Greco-Buddhist reliquary mound. The imaginative iconography demonstrates multiple influences in the animistic cult. Besides Celtic fairy faith, Greeks too represented the soul as a small winged human figure. However, soul or Ba represented as winged bird with human head originates in Egypt.

The mature period of the Indus Valley culture is reckoned to be 2600-1900 BC. It extended from northeast of Afghanistan to Pakistan and northwest India. The archaeological sites are mostly found on river banks, but also on the ancient seacoast, such as Balakot, and on islands, as in the case of Dholavira. Topography of Lothal too reflects its maritime past. To the northwest of Lothal lies the Kutch peninsula. Proximity to the Gulf of Khambhat allowed direct access to sea routes. The ruins of Harappa were first described in 1842 by Charles Masson in his *Narrative of Various Journeys in Balochistan, Afghanistan, and the Punjab,* where locals mentioned a dead city extending "thirteen cosses", which is about 25 miles. General Alexander Cunningham, the later Director General of the Archeological Survey of Northern India, visited Harappa in 1856 where the British engineers John and William Brunton were laying the East Indian Railway Company line connecting Lahore and Karachi. In the first publication of the Indus seal in 1872-75, Cunningham identified the Indus script as Brahmi letters. Brahmi, which unified a literate society in the Buddhist cult, was adapted from Aramaic and Greek letters. With the help of engineers Captain Edward Smith and George Turnour, James Prinsep had deciphered Brahmi only in 1837. Decades later Harappa was discovered and excavated by Sir John Hubert Marshall in 1921-22. By 1931, much of Mohenjo-Daro had been excavated by Marshall and others. In the light of mysterious gaps in the history of India, it was urgent to identify its prehistoric origins. The cryptic seals of the Indus Valley Civilization purposely veered away from the Brahmi theory. Yet, some scholars still consider Indus script significant to the development of Brahmi. According to Poschel, Iravatham Mahadevan and others, Tamil Brahmi as the forerunner claims Indus Valley Civilization as a unique feature of Dravidian identity.

Sir Mortimer Wheeler was sure that the un-deciphered pictographs alone did not merit its out-of-the-way distant past. Mohenjo-Daro crowned by a Buddhist reliquary stupa built of bricks followed the Roman Cardo in which the streets were laid out in straight lines North to South and at right angles to each other. Romans called the rectangular plots of building insulae in which the house clusters were planned and constructed like the so called Buddhist monasteries. Intrigued by the Roman type of brick work and drainage through corbelled arches, Sir Mortimer Wheeler, Director of the Archaeological Survey of India, renewed archaeological assessment of the structural remains in 1944. Cisterns and wells in Mohenjo-Daro were constructed of wedge-shaped bricks and the drains were made of terracotta pipes. Harappa in north Pakistan was built almost entirely of kiln-fired bricks. In general the bricks measure H.7 x W.14 x L.28 cm. All the bricks in the Indus Valley culture have the same ratio of 1:2:4 but were made in different sizes as required. Brick lined wells were common in Harappa, Chanhu-daro, and Lothal. Some of the brick lined wells in Mojenjo-Daro assumed unusual shapes. Besides an oval well, a heart shaped well in the Lower Town has been reconstructed in the Mohenjo-Daro Museum (1.31). A gold broach from Harappa in the same shape is ornamented with steatite beads capped with gold (1.31 inset).

1.31 Womb well, Lower Town, Mohenjo-Daro : Mohenjo-Daro Museum
Inset : Womb amulet in gold from Harappa, Length 2 ¼ in, Width 1 in, New Delhi: National Museum (49.254/4)

Votive objects in this distinctive womb-heart shape were fashioned in gold, shell, stone and other materials. The unusual symmetrical sign is similar to the traditional pretzel shape, without twisting back or intertwined dough ends of the loop. The womb or heart shape was equally significant in the Greco-Buddhist funerary cult in Gandhara. Exact type of womb-heart shaped votives are found in the burials of Tillya Tepe and Taxila reliquaries of the early Christian era (1.32 a, b). Is it possible that the Indus Valley Civilization is separated from the Buddhist reliquary cult by nearly two millennia of nothingness? Here hangs the key to the history of India. The incidence of the peculiar womb shaped amulet is such it suggests that the contiguity of the reliquary cults in the Indus Valley occurred not only in space but also in time datable to early Christian era. The womb-heart shape is naturally a bracelet as in the case of

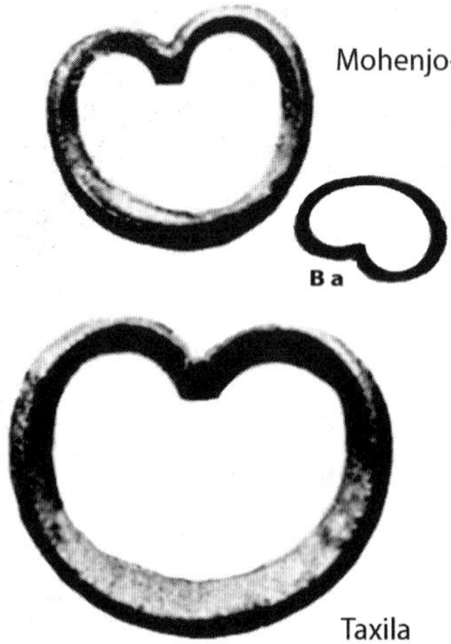

1.32a Womb amulet, Mohenjo-Daro and Taxila, Gandhara
Early historic period
1.32b Ba in the Tagalog Baybayin script, Philippines

Harappa shell bangles, which is common in Buddhist stupa sites as well.[11] The readily associated form of pretzels and its significance of renewed life at Easter within the Catholic Church might be actually linked to the primitive origins of ancient amulets of rebirth. Extending the associative cross-cultural memory further, the womb shape is letter "Ba" in the Tagalog Baybayin script in Philippines, which like all the Southeast Asian scripts comes from Brahmi derived from Aramaic (1.32b). Since "Ba" is Soul in Egyptian, the womb glyph in the multi-cultural milieu was probably metonymy for reincarnated dead, just as the rose representing the Rhodes Island in Greek means "field of rose."

BANADEVI THE TIGER GODDESS

In the cult of the goddess the tiger rules supreme in the Indus Valley. The most dramatic representation is the

1.33 Tiger and tree goddess, Terracotta, tablet, Mohenjo-Daro Proto-historic period
1.34 Deer bowl, Painted terracotta, Mohenjo-Daro

instant response of the tiger to the call of the goddess seated on a tree branch (1.33). An elephant stands on the other side of the molded terracotta. Rows of swift footed deer painted on a slip coated terracotta bowl records natural environment of the forest in sharp contrast to the hieratic form of the tiger, elephant and the one horned rhinoceros on the Indus seals and clay tablets (1.34).

Cheetah is derived from the word "Chita" for dots in Hindi and Urdu. Trained cheetahs were traditionally used in the royal hunts in Africa, Asia and India. Recently there is a growing demand for cheetahs as pets in the Gulf States. Up to two-thirds of the cheetah cubs smuggled across the war-torn Horn of Africa do not survive en route. The growing emphasis on big cat as luxury pet and status-symbol in the Middle East is not part of the health to wealth shift. In traditional medicine and magic rituals rhinoceros horns and tiger bones and body parts are still in demand. Rhinoceros and tiger like various other exotic animals are used as magical sign in the Indus Valley seals. Comparable to vignettes in Roman art, "Pashupati" on a Mohenjo-Daro seal is by now accepted as the Lord of Animal. When we reflect on the crested goddess in the Indus Valley culture, however, the sex change is quite obvious. The Mistress of

1.35 Tigress on leash, The Great Hunt mosaic, Villa Romana di Piazza Armerina, Sicily, Italy, ca. Ist-4th century AD

Animal is unmistakable in the depiction of the exceptional tiger-genius tiger-goddess.

Female empowerment comes from the forgotten depths of the forest. The strong female energy called 'Shakti' is traditionally the untamed nature spirit found in sacred forests and wild animals. Tiger is the earliest transport (Vahana) of the goddess that channels positive energy. From antiquity pelt of fierce felines, such as tiger and leopard used as clothing is considered mystical or divine symbol. Goddess Durga is Shakti worshiped as Banadevi and Banashankari (Ban/Van). Surrounded by the Tilakaraanya forest the Banashankari temple over-looks Agastya Lake in Karnataka. Located near Buddhist, Jain and Hindu cave temples at Badami, the tutelary deity of Chalukyan kings has been in worship from ancient times.

1.36 Tiger - Wild dog, Steatite, Mohenjo-Daro, Proto-historic period
1.37 Tiger-hippopotamus, Steatite seal, Mohenjo-Daro, Proto-historic period
1.38 Tiger-bull, Steatite seal, Mohenjo-Daro, Proto-historic period

During the annual Banashankari worship parents ritually ferry their newborn on boats made of banana stems in the temple tank. Banadevi known also as Budhi Pallien is worshiped across north India. Assamese in the northeast believe that the goddess roams with tigers, offers protection and communicates wisdom.

The jungle goddess is a shape shifter; she is believed to transform into a tiger. Among unusual tiger seals, a tiger stands in front of an offering tray. In another, the tiger is accompanied by a hunting dog (1.36). The tiger is a transformer. In one seal the tiger seems to combine the characteristics of hippopotamus (1.37). In another seal metamorphosis of the tiger is accomplished by hieroglyphic bull horns (1.38). In various cultures the bull alludes to god-king. The Egyptians invoked deified king as the "Bull in Heaven". The 'Tiger-bull' seems to unify the divine male-female aspects in nature. Here, the bull horns merged with the pictographic symbols adds to its meaning. According to Lucy Zuberbuhler, pictographic symbols in the Indus Script are most likely part of a logo-syllabic writing system. The Indus signs seem to represent syllables on some occasions and whole words or concepts on others, which would explain how some inscriptions could be so

1.39 Gilgamesh motif, Sandstone relief (in situ), Sanchi stupa, Mid 1st century AD

brief. In her PhD thesis "A comparison of the Kabul manuscript with the Indus script" Zuberbuhler keeps alive the possibility that the Indus Valley culture coexisted with the Buddhist cult during the Roman period.[12]

The cultural underpinnings of the Indus Valley depend on its relationship with other known cultures. The "Bull in Heaven" concept is intrinsic part of Mesopotamian Gilgamesh motif in which the culture hero overpowers lions. In a Sanchi stupa relief of the Greco-Kushana period, a man armed like an Assyrian king confronts a pouncing lion (1.39). Gilgamesh being only one part human and two parts divine, the unusual Buddhist relief glorifies an immortal King. The symbolic value of Gilgamesh known in Mohenjo-Daro is repeated in steatite tablets seal. On one side of a terracotta tablet molded on two sides a buffalo is speared as in a bull fight. The seated goddess turns her crested head to observe the ritual (1.40a). On the other side a naked woman dances with paired felines and together all look up at the hexagonal wheel overhead. Below is the

1.40a Spearing the bull, Molded tablet, Terracotta
1.40b Dance with animal, Obverse, Terracotta tablet

heavenly elephant transport (1.40b). In one of the seals a curly haired person that could be either male or female grapples two tigers with bare hands (1.41). In several other seals a female accomplishes the extraordinary feat of subduing tigers (1.42-44). In the Indus seals the Gilgamesh motif and the unfailing symmetrical composition is typically West Asian. The schematic composition in both cultures conveys immortality and apotheosis.[13]

Signs encoded language is peculiar to the Indus Valley in modern-day Pakistan, which was beyond the edge of the then known world. The Indian Ocean as the gateway to India defines a region of linguistic, ethnic, cultural and religious diversity. Surrounded by inaccessible mountainous and rivers the Indus Valley conducive for a mysterious but short-lived reliquary cult shares the characteristics of the Greco-Buddhist culture.[14] Symbols engraved in seals, pottery and various other materials were almost certainly for religious purpose; it communicated meaning to a large section of multilingual population. Lucy Zuberbühler thesis demonstrates that the script-symbols system was developed for a particular purpose, which according to researchers is religious.

Iconography points to the vital role of the goddess in afterlife. Consistently the learned society in Mohenjo-Daro shows preference for the divine female taming wild

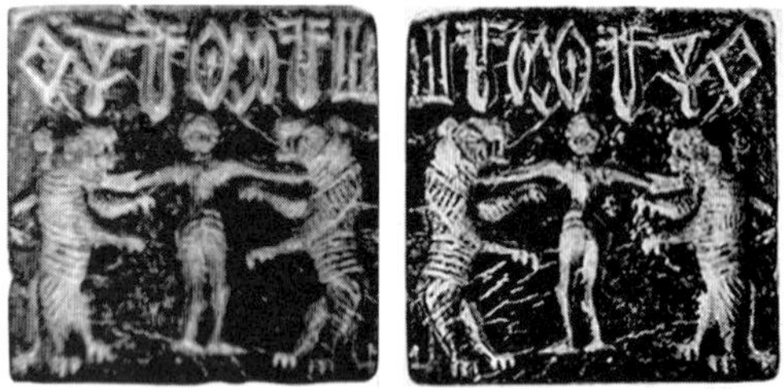

1.41 Gilgamesh motif, Steatite seal

1.42 Gilgamesh motif, Steatite seal and seal impression (Joshi/ Parpola, Corpus of Indus seals and inscriptions, Vol. 1, M 306).

1.43 Gilgamesh motif, Steatite seal

1.44 Gilgamesh seal and sealing, (Joshi/Parpola, Corpus of Indus seals and inscriptions, Vol. 1, M 307-8).

animals. Co-relating the tiger mosaics and seals might appear slanted. On the other hand, a lot of unexpected contexts open sideways that hopefully will act as a catalyst for further research. This approach should be carried out in the spirit of the panoramic way of thinking, searching for the reciprocity without which human beings do not develop. Lateral thinking is of crucial importance for mutual understanding. While dialectics assumed a two-division priori, in the conceptual world the main clue to the quadralectic communication is guided by a four-division system. The great aim will be 'to trace the place of the observer and the observed within the context of a fourfold communication' and evaluate the visible results.[15] In that context iconography in Indus Valley Civilization and Greco-Buddhist culture in terract with ancient Mediterranean and Celtic traditions. They all work together here like the fire, air, earth and water in nature that was brought together to guide the instinctive tetradic way of thinking.

REFERENCES

1. The Geography of Strabo published in Vol. I of the Loeb Classical Library edition, 1917: "At any rate, when Gallus was prefect of Egypt, I accompanied him and ascended the Nile as far as Syene and the frontiers of Kingdom of Aksum (Ethiopia), and I learned that as many as one hundred and twenty vessels were sailing from Myos Hormos to India, whereas formerly, under the Ptolemies, only a very few ventured to undertake the voyage and to carry on traffic in Indian merchandise."

2. All references to animal hunt during the Roman period are from Machinnon's "Supplying exotic Animals for the Roman Amphitheater Games." In: Historical and Ethnographic Data. Mouseion, Series III, Vol. 6 (2006) 1-25.

3. Machinnon, Michael. In : New Constructions combining Archaeological, Ancient Textual, Historical and Ethnographic Data. Mouseion, Series III, Vol. 6 (2006) 1-25. p.11.

4. http://www.careforthewild.com/what-we-do/campaigns/previous-campaigns/tiger-temple-the-truth/ Retrieved 2014 July 10

5. Elephant head fragment, Ptolemaic Faience, Circa 2nd century BC, Amsterdam: Collection of R. A. Lunsingh Scheurleer (581). Illustrated In: Pfrommer, Michael. *Metalwork from Hellenized East: Catalogue of the Collections of the J.Paul Getty Museum.* Calif.: J. Paul Getty Museum, 1993:16.

6. Muziris was an ancient seaport and urban center in south-western India that existed from around 1st century AD. Mentioned in Tamil (Muciri) literature and classical Greco-Roman historical sources, Muzuris might be located in the village of Pattanam near Cranganore. The 4th century Peutinger

Map (*Tabula Peutingeriana*) shows a temple to Augustus at Muziris.

7. In Indian tradition, tiger is the transport of Rahu, one of the nine planets (navagraha). Rahu's 'serpent bite' is believed cause the solar eclipse.

8. According to Rollin's Ancient History, the worship of Bacchus had been brought out of Egypt to Athens. Rollin, Charles. *The Ancient History of the Egyptians, Carthaginians, Assyrians, Babylonians, Medes and Persians, Grecians, and Macedonians*, Volume 1. 1839:388. (Google eBook)

9. Livingstone, David. The Dying God: The Hidden History of Western Civilization. iUniverse, 2002.

10. Dunbabin, Katherine M. D. *Mosaics of the Greek and Roman World.* Cambridge: Cambridge University Press, 2006: 92-94. 4th reprint.

11. The German "Brezel" may derive from Latin bracellus, a medieval term for "bracelet", or bracchiola meaning "little arms".

12. Lucy Zuberbuhler, 2009. http://www.indoeurohome.com/LucyZuberbuehler-indusscriptmss2009.pdf /Recovered 2014 July 20

13. Kenoyer, Jonathan Mark, *Ancient Cities of the Indus Valley*. Karachi, Oxford University Press and American Institute of Pakistan Studies, 1998: 114. Eschewing reciprocity, Kenoyer claims that the two cultures are unrelated.

14. Regarded as the early stages of civilization, the Indus Valley Civilization (2600–1900 BC) is referred to as the Indus or Harappan Civilization (Possehl 1996: 10-11).

15. Kuilman, Marten. Quadralectic Architecture: A Survey of Tetradic Testimonials in Architecture. Falcon Press, Heemstede, the Netherlands, 2011.

II

Indus Valley Seal – Goddess Bonabibi

Modern day India represents the largest democracy in the world with a seamless picture of unity in diversity unparalleled anywhere else.

Romain Rolland. *A Rough Guide to India.*

The Sundarbans is intersected by network of tidal waterways, mudflats and small islands of mangrove forests. Gangetic delta is harsh; fiery storms rip through periodically, sea water seeps into fresh water and solid earth slides under high tide. The Royal Bengal Tiger rules the Sundarbans spread across West Bengal and Bangladesh (2.1). South 24 Parganas district east of Kolkata battles the tides called Tharangamala or String of Waves and lives in constant fear of the tiger hungry for human flesh. South of Ganga estuary the tutelary deity of the mangrove forests is Bonabibi. River dolphins are the messengers of the goddess that rides the tiger.[1] Bonabibi, the Lady of the Forest, is worshiped by both Hindus and Muslims. Called variously as Bonbibi, Bandevi, Bandurga and Baghradevi, the sylvan goddess holds absolute power over the tiger. In the Sundarbans the dreaded word 'bagh' denotation tiger is never mentioned. Instead, the fierce king of the forest is propitiated as Dokhin Rai or Dakshina Thakura. The tiger cult confined to the South 24 Paragana district of West Bengal is dominated by supreme devotion to goddess Bonabibi and her brother Shah Jongoli. Both 'Jongol' and 'Bon' mean forest in Bengali. However, Bonabibi and Shah Jongoli originate neither in the Bay of Bengal nor in Hindu mythology. Although the forest entities are peculiar to the natural world of the Sundarbans, their story is tangled with West Asian culture and ancient maritime history. According to folklore the duo were born to the Sufi fakir Ibrahim (Abraham) in the Arabian city of Medina, the holiest city in Islam. The story begins with the banishment of his pregnant second wife, which is somewhat reminiscent of the story of Abraham in the Bible. Born in the wilderness, Archangel Gabriel transported the abandoned siblings to the remote delta region and set them on the divine mission to make the tiger and tide country fit for human habitation. Thus, Bonabibi and Shah Jongoli subdued and brought the Royal Bengal Tiger under their control. After a truce the demon tiger withdrew to the wilderness, respecting the boundaries of the human habitats.

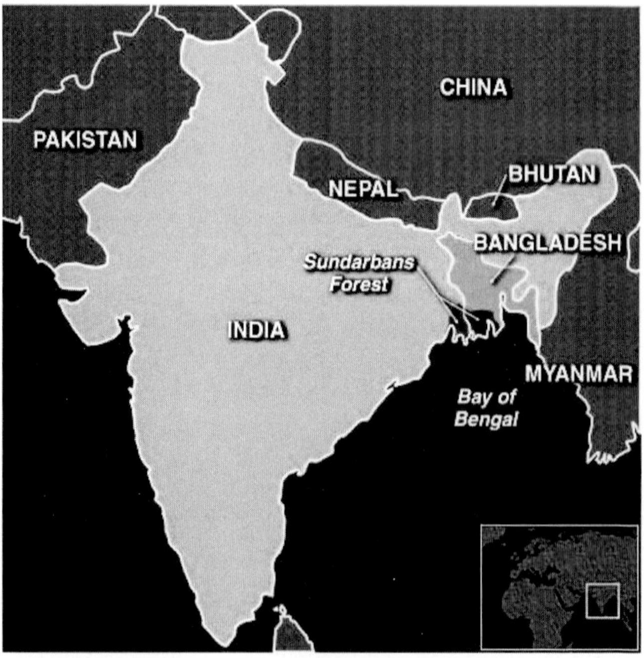

2.1 Map of Sundarbans

2.2 Royal Bengal Tiger in the Sundarbans, India
2.3 Tiger conservation in the Sundarbans, India

TIGER CULT IN BENGAL: Moon / Tide / Mud country

Characteristically, the tiger god is not always considered evil; Dokhin Rai when appeased is also looked upon as a benefactor. Reverential behavior towards the tiger is such that when it strays into a village, the tiger is caught and released in its sanctuary (2.2-3). Nonetheless, the delicate ecological balance in the Sundarbans is constantly threatened by human greed. Eroding coastline and poaching for commercial gain continually narrows the chances of survival for both man and beast. In this scenario, Bonabibi is the only savior. The ritual narrative of how Bonabibi saved the innocent youth Dukhey from the clutches of cunning men and the terrifying Dokhin Rai serves as an expression of faith in the magical power of the forest goddess. According to folklore, the encounter was first triggered by a greedy helmsman Dhona who entered Dokhin Rai's territory in search of forest treasures. The tiger king trapped Dhona and his crew in the forest. To escape Dokhin Rai's clutches Dhona agreed to deliver a poor boy named Dukhey as ransom. He fled with his men and abandoned Dukhey to be devoured by Dokhin Rai. When the tiger demon was about to pounce on the poor boy, Dukhey remembered his mother's advice to call upon Bonabibi in times of need. Instantly his appeal for deliverance was answered. Bonabibi appeared in a flash and sent the tiger back into the forest after chastising him.

2.4 Bonabibi and Shah Jongoli, Sundarbans (Photo Amitabh SenGupta)
2.5 Shrine of Bonabibi, Sundarbans, West Bengal, India
2.6 Icon of Bonabibi, Dukhey, Dokhin Rai, Sundarbans, India

In conclusion Dukhey was restored to his loving mother. This oft repeated story confirms faith in Bonabibi and Shah Jongoli committed to protect the devotees and maintain harmony in the world of nature. In local shrines, the goddess is dressed like a Bengali bride while Shah Jongoli usually retains his West Asian attire, footwear and beard (2.4). Bonabibi wearing a tiara is usually enthroned or is seated on a tiger (2.5). Typically the goddess is accompanied by Shah Jongoli and a diminutive youth called Dhukey the sorrowful, who personifies all the suffering humanity (2.6). No native in the Sundarbans will enter the jungle without seeking the blessings of Bonabibi. Ceremonial worship of the deity is usually performed in three different ways. It consists of daily worship, specific annual worship and special worship on behalf of the villagers. Blessing of Bonabibi is invoked by means of song recital accompanied by rituals and theatrical performances (2.7).

2.7 Bonbibir Pala, Glorification of Bonbibi
Sundarbans, West Bengal, India

2.8 Bonbibir Pala, Dukhey's struggle with tiger demon
Sundarbans, West Bengal, India

2.9 Goddess of the Wild, Steatite seal, Mohenjo-Daro, Proto-historic period
2.10 Tiger and the sylvan goddess, Steatite seal, Mohenjo-Daro, Proto-historic period

2.11 Tiger and the sylvan goddess, Steatite seal, Mohenjo-Daro, Proto-historic period
2.12 Tiger and the sylvan goddess, Steatite seal, Mohenjo-Daro, Proto-historic period

All year round and particularly during the annual worship of Bonabibi, local theatre companies called 'jatra-dol' in Bengali travel from village to village to glorify Bonabibi by enacting her popular narrative. The tiger king called Dokhin Rai has vivid representation in the jatra. Fear of the tiger is so overwhelming that pronouncement of 'Bagh' (tiger) is taboo (2.8).

2.13 Tree-Cow goddess and tiger god, Steatite seal, Mohenjo-Daro, Proto-historic period

2.14 Lotus medallion, Sandstone, 1st-2nd century AD, Bodh Gaya, Bihar

According to legend Dakkhin Rai ruled the land of the eighteen tides in the south before Bonabibi and her brother arrived on the scene. The tiger king and his legion under the rule of the forest goddess fade into the beginning of time. If we observe closely, number of Indus Valley seals seems to illustrate scenes from the Bonabibi folk epic. First, the goddess of the wild seated in hieratical posture carries her distinctive identity on her crown (2.9). Further, the tiger responds submissively to the forest goddess represented on a tree (2.10-12). The peculiar 'Turn Back' posture of the tiger by itself is significant means to convey invisible power of the divine female. The backward gaze of animals was a popular device in Central Asian silk that protected the departed. The goddess dancing with the tiger in another seal demonstrates the climax of accord reached by the goddess and the tiger king (2.13). Horns of the goddess might allude to her connection with the moon according to which the tide country moves and responds. It is during the full moon that Bonabibi receives exceptional worship. However, the eloquent description of the goddess with bovine tail and hoof together with cow horns is theriomorphic form of Egyptian mother goddess Isis-Hathor. Described as the "Great Flood" the cow goddess protects the living and nourishes the dead in afterlife.

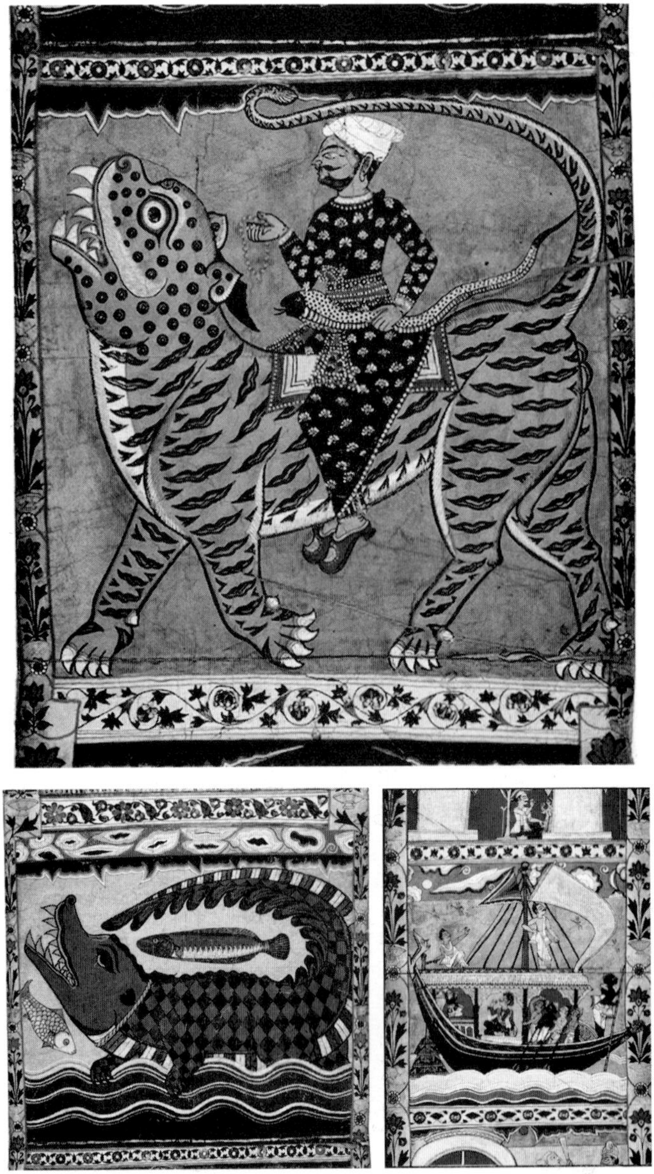

2.15a-c The Legend of Gazi, Scroll painting, Unknown artist, London: The British Museum, Purchased through the Art Fund Asia (OA 1955.10-8.095)

2.16 Prismatic tablet, Terracotta, Mohenjo-Daro, Bronze Age, Proto-historic period
2.17 Terracotta tablet, Mohenjo-Daro, Bronze Age, Proto-historic period

TIGER PSYCHOPOMP: Legend of Gazi Pir / Sufi mysticism

Leaping tiger and deer in a lotus medallion from Bodh Gaya stupa describes natural environment of the Sundarbans (2.14). The lotus of rebirth conveys immortality, which was attained by Gazir Pir invoked as the ‘Living Saint’ (Zenda / Zindah Ghazi) revered along with Bonabibi in the Sundarbans. Gazi Pir, also called Satya Pir, can control untamed forces of nature and protect his devotees from tiger, snake, crocodile and other wild animals (2.15a-c). Sundarbans comes alive in a molded prismatic terracotta tablet from Mohenjo-Daro. The inscribed votive depicts boat of salvation carrying the ‘bird soul’ and crocodile happily feasting on fish (2.16). Similar terracotta votive from Mohenjo-Daro depicts serpents and humans adoring a seated divine being (2.17). The narrative scroll painting glorifying the medieval Saint Zenda Gazi in the Sundarbans follows same pattern. Local people pray to Gazi Pir for his protection while they go about their job in the perilous jungle. The Muslim saint seems to be a fearless lieutenant of Bonabibi who set out with the same divine mission at the height of Sufi mysticism in the 15th century India. Most probably he appeared during the reign of Sultan Barbak Shah (1459-1474) when Orissa (Odisha) and Kamrup (Assam) came under his domain. According to a local legend Gazi Pir or Ghazi Saheb had power over dangerous animals. He made them harmless and transformed them into gentle creatures. He rode a fearsome Bengal tiger while holding a poisonous snake in his hand (2.15a). Through his amazing

2.18 The Legend of Gazi, Scroll painting, Unknown artist, Kolkata: Amitabha SenGupta Collection

2.19a Confusing the tiger with mask, Honey collector Madhusudhan Mondal, Bali village, Sundarbans

2.19b Honey collectors wearing mask board a boat, Gosaba Island, Sundarbans (Photo Suzanne Lee)

influence over the harmful creatures, he made it possible for people to live peacefully and farm the inhospitable jungle fearlessly. Cult of Bonabibi and Gazi Pir unifies the local people irrespective of caste, creed and religion. Itinerant storytellers in rural Bengal use long narrative scroll-painting as visual aid to illuminate local myths. Gazi scroll paintings (Gazir Pot/Pat/Patachitra) illustrate astonishing events in the life of Gazi Pir, such as receiving the homage of tigers, clash with demons, controlling the tide and the dangerous animals and curiously making cows give milk miraculously (2.18).

Sundarbans is populated mostly by low caste Hindu and Muslim communities engaged in farming, fishing and collecting honey and wood in forest. When men venture into the forest they appeal to Bonabibi and set forth with magical incantations taught by Gazi Pir. They also try to shield themselves with mask worn at the back of the head to confuse the tiger that normally pounces on the exposed neck and kills its prey (2.19a). It is interesting to note that the mask represents either the Gazi Pir or bearded Shah Jongoli (2.19b). It seems to be an additional safety device since Shah Jangali takes on Dakkhin Rai at the swift command of Bonabibi while Gazi Pir is ever present to offer protection.

Recently in the vast mangrove forest sixty-two year old Sushil Majhi was fishing in a creek. He was with his son and daughter when a Bengal tiger pounced on his neck, swung his body on to its back, and leapt out of the boat and disappeared into the forest. Majhi's children tried to scare the tiger with a stick and in vain gave chase through the mangrove. In response to their alarm other fishermen rushed to the spot, but did not dare to venture into the woods. The chance of recovering Majhi's body is unlikely. Within six months of this report the fourth such attack happened in 2014. The man had reportedly ventured into a prohibited area at dawn, making him all the more vulnerable. Divisional Forest Officer of South 24 Parganas district Lipika Roy regretted that the unfortunate incident was the result of trespassing into the "big cat" (Bada bidal) territory. Each time the tiger kills, it is thus customary to hold the man accountable in the belief that the tussle with the demon king is aggravated by the man's misjudgment and mistakes.

Nowadays villages are protected by nylon net fencing so that tigers straying into populated areas are fewer. However, life in the forest is hard and relentless. Tiger and crocodile attack together with snake bite has reduced some villages to grieving womenfolk so that certain villages are known as the 'Widow Village'. In this scenario only folk deities give solace and serve as powerful front against all danger. In ritual worship married women assume widowhood in the belief that Bonabibi would protect their menfolk and relieve them from such pitiful condition. Customarily, while waiting for the safe return of their husbands, they surrender to the forest goddess auspicious symbols such as sindur (vermillion powder), sankha and pala (white shell and red bangles). To intensify their fervent appeal they go into mourning and do not cook during the daytime. They have the surety that Bonabibi would listen to their appeal and rekindle their hearth fire. Frequently they shrill musical appeals to Bonabibi on the sea shore and rivulets and seek protection for their men. Upon their safe return the villagers gather together with the catch of fish and dance to the accompaniment of drums to praise the kind hearted Bonabibi. The men relate their desperate plight in fishing boats rocked by storm and their encounter with death when they came face to face with the tiger. And they recall with awe how Bonabibi saved them from the tiger and the turbulent waves when they cried plaintively "Bonabibi….. Bonabibi."

The immensely powerful Bonabibi is worshipped on the full moon day in the Bengali months Chitra (March-April), Baisakh (April-May), Poush (December-January) and Magha (January-February). The annual worship of Bonabibi takes place on the last Tuesday (Mongalbar) of Baisakh (April-May) When after a week of fasting and praying women perform Manat Puja for wish fulfillment. The annual ritual is performed at a specific cult site called 'Bonabibir Than' on the eastern river bank. Here a temporary shrine is erected in bamboo and thatch made of coconut leaves. The make-shift shrine is raised on stilts to protect from the rising tide. The image of goddess Bonabibi is then ceremoniously installed for worship. Usually a banana sapling as auspicious sign of the goddess is planted next to the shrine. In folk tradition the village shrine is always located by a sacred tree.

It is possible to recollect the past through the present. In an Indus sealing we come across the forest goddess enshrined under ornamental archway (Torana) that resemble coconut or palm leaves folded in a decorative manner (2.20). Similar torana made of tender coconut leaves sanctifies a site prepared for a shrine. Fishermen, crab-hunters and local people from nearby villages cross the river in groups to gather at the Bonabibi shrine for the annual worship. With the release of a hen into the wild, early morning rituals begin at the sacred 'Than' (site). Womenfolk cook rice and milk porridge in new earthen pots as

2.20 Shrine of goddess, terracotta sealing, Mohenjo-Daro, Bronze Age, Proto-historic period

2.21 Goddess and tiger in a ritual scene, Terracotta, Sealing (M-478 B) Proto-historic period, Mohenjo-Daro

offering to the goddess. Although the worship is Hindu in nature the ritual always begin with the Islamic invocation 'Bismillah'. The story of Bonabibi is then recited to the reverent gathering as integral part of worship. After the puja people return to their villages in the afternoon. An annual Jungle Fair (Jungaler Mela) on the occasion is held at the nearby Nagenabad village on the western bank of the river. The fair starts in the afternoon of a Tuesday and continues for the next seven days. In the manner of a narrative scroll, the terracotta sealing from Mohenjo-Daro seems to depict the cult rituals connected to the forest goddess and the tiger god of the Sundarbans (2.21). Bonabibi and Dokhin Rai in folk style represents composite image of the forest goddess seated on the tiger god. A painting in the unique style of Mithila or Madhubhan in the neighboring State of Bihar demonstrates conventional worship offered in the natural environment of the forest (2.22).

2.22 Bonabibi and tiger, Madhubani painting, 20th century, Unknown artist, Bihar, India

General belief in forest spirits, firm faith in the fakirs and superstitious customs even among Muslims is a matter of surprise to outsiders. The ethnographic inquiry of popular religion has fascinated early observers of the Sundarbans. Bankim Chandra Chatterjee has featured Sundarban prominently in his novel *Kapal Kundla*. Of particular interest are the intermediaries on whom the people depend to protect themselves. The tiger is exorcised by fakir or 'geanee', the wise-man conferred with power over tigers. Hunters and honey and wax gatherers venture into the forest invariably accompanied by a fakir who provides protective amulets and recites magical incantations to lock the jaws of fierce tigers or dispel the tigers out of their away. For instance, before entering the forest, the exorcist calls out to Bonabibi and establishes a tiger-free area that extends over the territory covered by the sound of his voice. A Mohammedan fakir is of great interest; he is easily recognized by his quick intelligence, sharp eyes and wild demeanor. He exerts great influence over men who regularly risk their lives to extract forest yield. Not a man will step out of his boat and enter the jungle unless preceded by a fakir; not a follower or a beater will join a hunting party unless services of a geanee is enlisted. The fakir exorcists with considerable shamanistic powers recite various magical words to restrain tigers from entering human zone while still others inflict a burning sensation on the great cats, causing them to flee. The symbiatic relationship between Hindus and Mohammedans in the Sundarbans, as during the Mughal period, reveals how the two cultures overlap and mutually alter and reshape each other.

GANGARIDAI : Legend / Shape shifter / Raising the dead

The vast Sundarbans, the intermittently submerged archipelago covered by vast mangrove forests forms the delta of the Ganges as the river flows irresistibly into the Bay of Bengal. The "24 Paragana" of Bengal was first recorded by Abu al-Fazal ibn Mubarak in Ain-i-Akbari (1596). Earlier the Romans mapped the region near the area of Adi Ganga as "Gangaridee" (2.23). Moving with the wind and the tides the ancient mariners once traversed the imaginary boundaries of the modern nation-states, where the mouths of the many river-channels set up a unique turbulence of fresh and salt water lapping the islands that appear and disappear. Sundarbans covered with dense forest of mangrove trees is replete with anecdotes of wars between local kings. It was also the gateway of pirates known as Harmads and Mugs of Portuguese or Arakanese origin. Their atrocities

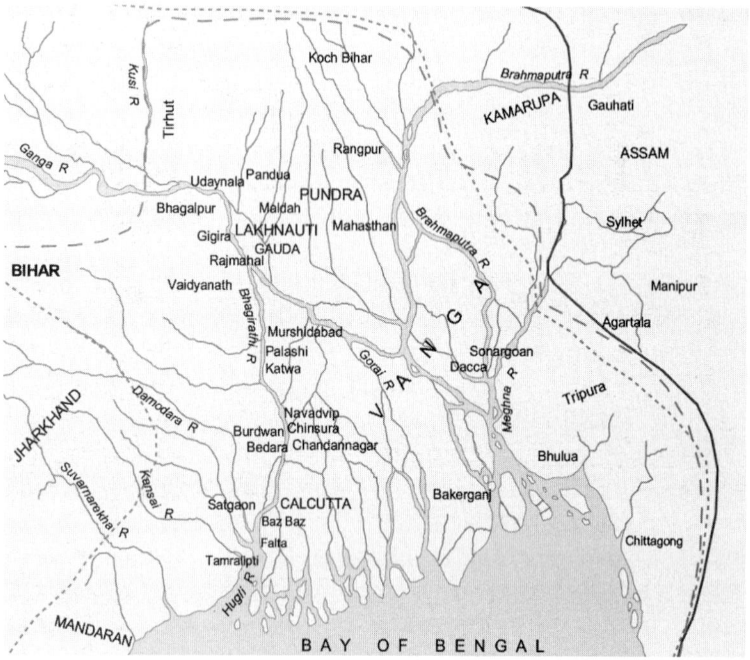

2.23 Confluence of Ganges and Brahmaputra, Tamralipti or Tamluk Archaeological site in the Bay of Bengal, Sundarbans.

reverberate with cries of slaughtered natives and wails of women shipped to foreign shores.

The swampy land known as the 'Sundarbans' is the 'beautiful forest' named after the sundari tree, as the mangrove tree is locally called. The complex ecosystem of Sundarbans stretches across three largest tracts of mangrove forests of the world. Two-thirds of the Sundarbans is in Bangladesh, only one-third is in India. The seaward fringe of the Sundarbans delta in India and in Bangladesh side of the border is listed separately in the UNESCO world heritage as the Sundarban National Park and the Sundarbans respectively. The oral and literary traditions derive from the ecosystem of east and west Sundarbans are not separated along the line of this division. Both have shared elements along the coastlines that unite them in the folklore of Chand-Saodagar, Behula-Lakshindar, Gazi or Satya

2.24 River goddess Ganga, Kalighat painting, 19th century, West Bengal
2.25 River Goddess Ganga, Amaravati, 2nd century AD, London: The British Museum

Pir and Atteshwar. However, cult of Bonabibi rooted in the forest to the east differs from the legend of Gangasagar in the west.

The river dolphin Orcalla bevirostris and crocodile is transport of the river goddess. The vahana of Ganga is synthesized makara-yali that displays characteristics of both dolphin and crocodile (2.24). River goddess glorified in Greco-Buddhist reliquary cult is the Mistress of Animal. She guarantees fertility, protection and heavenly bliss (2.25). East of Kolkata, Tamluk in the Greco-Roman period was once cult centre of the goddess, whose origins is lost in the annals of antiquity. Ancient votive terracotta from Tamluk (Tamaralipta) and other related sites in the delta region indicate thriving goddess cult (2.26). In the distant past pilgrims seeking refuge from the fury of primal nature surrendered to the goddess in the sacred groves of the sundari trees. Beset by unpredictable tiger and tide, their volatile life gained stability under the gaze of the goddess. Chandraketugarh is about 35 km northeast of Kolkata in the district

2.26 Goddess shrine, Terracotta, H.26.7 x W.20 cm, Ohio : Cleveland Museum of Art (1990.281) Florence and Herbert Irving Gift

of 24 Parganas of West Bengal where the tiger goddess emerges from the distant past in votive terracotta (2.27). Datable to early Christian era the site has wide variety of reliquary deposits. These include ritually buried punch-marked silver and copper coins, blank copper tokens, terracotta plaques and figurines of the goddess. The punch-marked bhuta (Bhuda) or ghost coins in the reliquary deposits have various symbols. Among these, bird,

2.27 Mistress of Animals, 1st-2nd century AD, Kolkata: Asutosh Museum, University of Calcutta
2.28 Funerary urn, Terracotta, H.28 cm, D. 13.5 cm, 1st-2nd century AD, Chandraketugarh

elephant, sun, cross, and six-armed signs indicate close contact with the Greco-Buddhist site Taxila in the Indus Valley region of modern Pakistan. Earthen wares include roulette Roman pottery, long necked jar, amphorae shards, big rimless round cups and bowls, fragments of ivory and copper antimony rods, and a large number of beads, seals and sealing. Terracotta funerary urns from the Sundarbans depict ritual worship of the goddess. In one of the urns, the winged goddess surrounded by lotus blossoms holds dagger in her hands (2.28).

As the local population continuously struggle against the tiger and the tide, Sundarbans' legend begins with Bhagirath Muni who released Ganges from Gangotri in the Himalayas. From the lake high in the western Himalayas River Ganga flows through the plains of northern India and arrives at its confluence in the Sundarbans. The tiger and the tide country marks the estuarine phase of the Ganges as well as the Brahmaputra river systems. It is said that to take a dip in the Sagara where Ganga embraces the sea in thousand forked streams is equal to ten horse sacrifice known as Ashvamedha Yagna. Narada explains in the Ramayana the circumstances that made the Bay of Bengal sacred. Devaraja Indra had hidden King Sagara's sacrificial horse underground in the Patal of the Sundarbans. The horse was concealed next to Kapila muni's hermitage. The 'sixty thousand sons' of King Sagara searching for the horse descended into the netherworld and rudely disturbed the meditating sage. As a result Kapila muni reduced them to ashes and consigned them to hell. Afterwards the sage relented and on his advice Bhagiratha, the sole surviving grandson of Sagara, brought River Ganga to liberate their hapless soul on the day of Makara Sankranti (15th January). Gangasagar in the archipelago of the Sundarban is thus acknowledged a holy site in which the enduring myth of redemption gives stability to a region where islands vanish and the land underfoot is engulfed by waves in an instant. Ascetics, Naga sadhus and pilgrims come to wash away sin at the birth of New Year on 15th January. When the Sun reenters Capricorn. The renewal of faith in rebirth is now capitalized by temple builders and imported priests.[2] The confluence of River Ganga has been fundamental to the religious belief of the people where they continue to come in droves to embrace the lap of the river goddess with the hope that their soul will be released to eternal bliss. Cult of Bonabibi co-exists with this endless cycle of renewal that takes place in the Sundarbans.

REFERENCES

1. Ghosh, Amitav. *The Hungry Tide*. New Delhi: Harper-Collins Publishers India, 2005:234. Fifth Reprint.

2. Jaduram, Zamindar of Sagardwip, migrated from Midnapur and built the present temple in 1974. He appointed a priest from Hanuman Garhi in Ayodhya. Eventually the

Ayodhya sect took over the temple so that Hanuman with the healing touch of Gandhamadan hill is represented in the shrine along with Ganga devi on makara, Bhagaban Kapil, Raja Sagar, Lord Indra and Durga on lion.

III

Bonabibi Pala – Folk Epic

If there is one place on the face of earth where all the dreams of living men have found a home from the very earliest days when man began the dream of existence, it is India.

Romain Rolland. *A Rough Guide to India.*

Folk Epic of the Tiger in the Tide Country comes from the Sundarbans delta where River Ganga meets the sea. The folk epic of Bonabibi is derived from the oral traditions of Sundarbans, the Beautiful Forest.[1] Sundarbans consists of Extraordinary landscape of about a hundred islands through which the river makes a network. It is not only the tiger but also the snake and the crocodile in these waters that pose danger when on an average the water level dramatically changes ten feet between high tide and low tide. The amazing natural event daily submerges land masses and creates new ones. So the trees in mangrove forests go under water and roots grow upwards to breathe air.[2] The Irrawady dolphin as messenger of Bonabibi is a sign of redemption to those living in this netherworld. Legends about the savior goddess has produced a folk epic based on oral narrative tradition.[3] Known as Bona Bibi Pala the ballad glorifies goddess Bonabibi who saves fatherless Dhuke the Sorrowful. The epic narrative in poetic form has set conventions. At the center is the hero who battles for survival while his companions face dreadful moral conflicts that challenges the very core of humanity. Dhuke at best represents the anti-hero; the puny helpless boy's only redeeming quality is his

3.1 Sylvan goddess and tiger god, Steatite seal, circa 2700-2000 BC, Mohenjo-Daro, Proto-historic period

unfailing faith in Bonabibi. Absolute faith in the forest goddess reflects the issues of a civilization teetering on the edge of untamed nature. The sylvan goddess transforms the dreadful savage tiger into awesome natural force worthy of reverence. In that sense the folk epic evolved from the life experience in the inhospitable jungle is uniquely attuned to ecology.

Dakshin Raya chasing Dukhe is a virtual nightmare that haunts villagers their entire lifetime. In the folk epic, Dukhe took leave of his widowed mother and accompanied his uncle Dhonai and his boatmen in a fleet of seven boats on an expedition to the forest to collect honey and wax. In the forest the predicament of Dukhe's uncle Dhonai was difficult. He would lose his boat, his companions and all his accumulated wealth of honey and wax if he did not offer Dukhe to the devouring Dakshin Raya. At first Dhonai tried to appease the tiger god with sweets, incense and perfume as prescribed on a Saturday ritual. When he failed to satisfy Dakshin Raya the uncle abandoned Dukhe to his fate. The hapless boy had no one to turn to except Bonabibi since his mother had impressed upon him the glory of the all powerful forest goddess. At Dukhe's call Bonabibi materialized instantly and with the help of Shah Jangali subdued and transformed the tiger into her obedient transport. The dance of the sylvan goddess with the tiger god is a supernatural vision recorded in the Indus seals (2.13, 3.1). Scarred by tiger attack, honey collector Balai Das' real life story is unbelievable. Miraculously he is alive to tell how Bonabibi saved him from the jaws of a tiger.[4] This is in the heart of all those who pray to Bonabibi seated majestically on the tiger demon. Theatrical performances that manifest the goddess illustrate the role of oral tradition in local religion. Furthermore, Bonabibi Pala is ever expanding saga knitting various stories relating miraculous escapes and tragic encounters that always result from human shortcoming. Although grounded in reality, miserable humans rise above their dreadful day to day lives – protective saints help them gain strength, wisdom and values.

EPIC FANTASY : Magic / Quest / Cult / Ritual

Tiger god Dakshina Raya sought Zenda Pir's shelter when he was battered by Shah Jangali, Bonabibi's brother in arms. In the Muslim legend Ghazi Pir rides a tiger and Dakshina Raya is one of his tiger followers (3.2). The patron-saint of wood-cutters protects them from tigers and crocodiles (3.3). Zindah Ghazi from Zindik-i-Ghazi is the Conqueror of Infidels. Ghazi Pir is sometimes identified with Ghazi Mian or Ghazi Madar. He is also confused with Badiruddin Shah Madar who died in A. H. 840 fighting against the infidels.[5] Songs are sung in his honor and offerings are made after a safe return from the forest. Hindu women often make vows to have songs sung in his honor when their children reach a certain age. An earthen mound represents Ghazi Pir. His shrine is believed to be on a mountain called Madaria in the Himalayas. Then again, Ghazi Saheb is identified with Zenda or Zindah Ghazi. Zenda and his brother Kalu are Musalman saints (pirs) who exercise absolute power over all living things and possess the ability to protect all those they love. They could command tigers to come to them or to walk away

3.2 Canopied shrine, Votive terracotta, Chandraketugarh, 1st century AD, Private collection

3.3 Man riding alligator, Votive terracotta, Chandraketugarh, 1st century AD, Private collection

and disappear into thin air. It is further alleged that they ride on tigers and rove about in the jungle. Hence the tiger is called "Ghazi's horse."

The revered Muslim saint Zenda Ghazi offers protection to the people of Sundarbans. On their behalf the fakirs pray to Ghazi Saheb and his brother Kalu and recite the following incantation to avert tiger attack:

> "Ghazi Saheb, you are a fakir. As a fakir, I fall at thy feet and plead. You have come to these jungles with 300 tigers. I beg you to shut the mouth of tigers."
>
> "Kalu you are brother of Ghazi. I salute you in his name and ask for your help. If you should injure me after this salutation, you shall die and burn in hell. I beg you to shut the mouth of tigers."

Trust in the Pir is absolute. Dakshina Raya is part of the tiger troupe that follows the Mahomedan Saint Zenda. When a Musalman or a Hindu living in that part of the country ventures into the jungle, he first of all bows down to the earth. And joining together the palms of his hands before his face, mumbles the words: "In the name of the Ghazi Saheb." After this prayerful act he enters the forest with the assurance that the saint will protect him.[6] Bonabibi Pala (Ballad) too discloses a curious mixture of Muslim and Hindu beliefs and customs. When Dukhe falls down senseless, Bonabibi invokes the Powerful Name of Allah and restores him by blowing over his body. The tiger god Dakshina Raya having been punished by Bonabibi seeks the shelter of another Muslim Saint Zenda Ghazi and in the end acknowledges his subordination to both. Ghazi Pir heals Dakshina Raya by lightly rubbing his wounds with his hands while pronouncing the Powerful Name of Allah. From the foregoing we get glimpses of Mahomedan method of exorcism by either lightly rubbing or blowing on the body while uttering the Powerful Name of Allah. The same method is used by fakirs to cure snake or scorpion venom. Hindu exorcist follows the same method to the accompaniment of mantra or magical incantations seeking the help of various deities.[7]

Another way of protecting oneself is never to utter "bagh", for the word is swifter than deer and can manifest the fearsome beast in an instant. The "big cat" is ever present in their midst. Everyone knows someone who has been attacked or killed by the tiger. Even when out of sight, the tiger is secretly watching all those who go about their livelihood - collecting honey or fire wood. Catching shrimp and crab at the crack of dawn expose them to daily risk. When they enter small rivulets to fish they are defenseless and vulnerable in their small boat. Honey and wax gatherers offer worship on a Saturday with offerings of sweets, incense and perfume. Interestingly the Muslim boatman Dhonai in the ballad performs the same Hindu rites to propitiate the tiger god. Katha-Vachana is living tradition in India. Chanted narrative can take different shape and different directions. Several versions of Bonabibi Pala (Ballad) are familiar to the Bengali audiences. In one version the tiger god Dakshina Raya is a powerful man. He reportedly killed countless tigers and crocodiles with bow and arrow and other weapons. On another occasion he defeated the tigers with bare hands. It is for this reason that as "the Lord of the 18 Ehalis" Dakshina Raya personified as the tiger. Worshipped to the present day by low caste Hindus and Muslims living in the Sundarbans, the regional caste based cult grants unity in diversity.

INDUS AND BMAC: Bridging Worlds / Development / Spread

The central question is about the tiger king. Dakshina Raya denotes 'King of the South' and in this context it refers to the watery netherworld south of Sundarbans. The tiger king impersonates a despotic chieftain displaying elemental predisposition and unrestrained power. The demonic king (rakhosh) in the guise of a man eating tiger justified his act as taxation (kar). People living in his domain have to pay with their lives for the forest yield he assumes ownership. The beautiful mangrove forest (adaon) is called Land of eighteen tides (Athero bhatir desh). In this tide and tide country Dhukhe is literally personified "grief". To save Dhukhe the forest goddess Bonabibi brings the tiger under her control and transforms the tiger king as her transport. We find that in the Indus seals the forest goddess is in harmony with the tiger that responds to her call. In the dance with the tiger the divine female and the tiger actually become one in the Indus seal. Archaeologists have long puzzled over the origin of exceptional artifacts inscribed in Indus script (3.4). It was equally mystifying to Victor Sarianidi and his team to recover from the Oxus palace citadel of Gonur an elephant seal inscribed in Indus hieroglyphs (3.5).

It is interesting to note that Damir District in the Indus Valley was formerly known as Yaghestan, the Land of the Free and the Unconquerable Rebel. While the Indus script is yet to be deciphered, a recent study at the Tata Institute of Fundamental Research (TIFR) and University of Mumbai suggests that the Indus writing wasn't homogenized. Indications are that distinct group of people used the inventive script for magical purpose in an obsolete cult. Gonur is type site of BMAC (Bactria Margiana Archaeological Complex) extending over parts of northern

3.4 Elephant seal, Indus Valley, Proto-historic period
3.5 Elephant seal, Oxus Gonur site, Bactria-Margiana Archaeological Complex, Bronze Age, Turkmenistan
Archaeology Victor Sarianidi, 2006. Photo Kenneth Garrett

Afghanistan, Turkmenistan, southern Uzbekistan, Tadjikistan, eastern Iran and Baluchistan. Archaeological remains in Gonur Tepe are dated to about 2500 to 1500 BC. Gonur citadel in Turkmenistan and Indus sites in Pakistan has several parallels. For unknown reasons abrupt rejection of this funerary cult seems to have led to the abandonment of the sites. The forsaken relics in these sites are fossil type that played no role in the development of subsequent national cultures. In the absence of textual sources, integrative analyses of anthropological and archaeological material is rewarding in reconstructing the lost civilization and the role of animals in antiquity.

Among more than thousand pieces of burial goods the tiger was deemed the perfect spirit medium in the tomb of Western Han Nanyue king (203 BC - 111 BC). As symbol of metamorphosis the Han king accepted the sinuous tiger as his escort to heaven (3.5). The bronze tiger inlaid in gold flame like stripes is inscribed: 'The king orders the carriage to move.' The plump tiger identified by its flame like stripes appears in the Indus Valley seals (1.20). The Gonur tiger plaque with similar flaming stripes is carved in greenish gray chlorite that is similar to steatite (3.6). The tiger standing on a base is realistically

3.6 Bronze tiger, Inscribed and inlaid with gold, 203 BC - 111 BC, Western Han, China

3.7 Tiger, Chlorite or steatite, L.3.6 cm, Oxus Gonur site (BMAC), Turkmenistan, Archaeology Victor Sarianidi. Norbert Schirnmel Loan, New York: The Metropolitan Museum of Art (L.1983.119.24)

modeled in relief. Its head turned forward is sculpted fully in the round.[8] Due to presence of mica chlorite naturally has glassy luster but the three-dimensional relief is in addition covered with gold leaf. The stripes are inlaid with precious variegated stones. Carved almost certainly from actual observation of the animal, such relief sculpture is unusual for Central Asia. Currently, this object along with the Indus Valley seals in the naturalistic intercultural style is dated to the Bronze Age. However, in the relatively short-lived prehistoric cultures proper time is a matter of speculation.

How this fantastic tiger entered the mythology of western Central Asia is not known. Iconography in the Central Asian glyptic is full of powerful heroes dominating or almost mastering the dangerous forces embodied by lions, snakes and winged dragons. The culture hero balancing tigers is exceptional in the Indus seals. The tiger identified by its flame like stripes is rarely seen in the art of Mesopotamia or Iran but commonly appears in Central Asian burial silk and in the intaglio seal of Mohenjo-Daro. The closest comparison is the feline on an impressive bronze axe with silver inlay reportedly from the North-West Frontier Province of India now in the British Museum. It has stripes indicated by an interlocking S-pattern. The tiger has the same features as the

3.8 Gold seal, Han China, 1st century AD

Gonur plaque such as wedge-shaped nose and round cheeks. The unusual early historic bronze axe depicts row of animals in which a boar follows a tiger that attacks a goat like antelope.[9] The lack of any other references makes it impossible to understand the meaning of this elaborate axe. If anything, this demonstrates that in the crossroads of cultures Bonabibi Pala and the legend of Zenda Kazi in the later India ride on this foundation of cross-cultural medley.

In antiquity cult of the tree goddess and the tiger god was apparently worldwide. Geographical expansion was probably through oral tradition, which spread as a reaction to different religious contexts and racial groups.[10] The study of history through genetics in the Northern Silk Road introduces "genetic archaeology". Tocharians are a genetic mixture of Caucasian and Asian haplotypes found among Celts. In genetic archaeology we cannot overlook the Celtic rune similar to Chinese or Indus Valley script that held phonetic value enriched and altered by its symbolic meaning (3.7). We know for sure that Celts consecrated a Greco-Buddhist reliquary monument at Sanchi in Central India (1.30a, b). The conical hat of Celts in Sanchi relief might designate a Druid. Loulan burials in Tarim Basin offer valuable clues to a lost civilization. Among the grave goods feathered conical hat of the 'Loulan Beauty' might be a sign of female shaman. Besides wooden comb and colored divination sticks, shamans were buried with small woven cloth or felt bags filled with medicinal herbs including cannabis and herbs prized

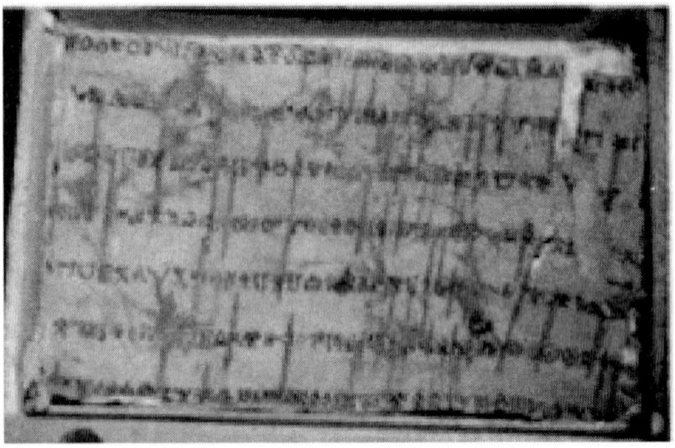

3.9 Indus script, Birch bark Kabul MS, Afghanistan, Vienna Facsimile: Western Himalaya Archive (SNO5 1000, 7081)

for magical qualities. Some of the mummies wear clothes similar to the clan plaids of northern Scotland. The 'Cherchen Man' is a mummy from the Taklamakan Desert discovered near Qiemo (Cherchen). The Cherchen Man is one among several other Caucasian men and women buried in the Xinjiang Uighur Autonomous Region. Their remains are a reminder of the voyage taken by Celts into the Taklamakan desert. In the language of the local Uighur people, "Taklamakan" means "You come in and never come out." The fate of the Cherchen Man and several other Celts like him was sealed when they traveled from Europe to Central Asia. And spreading across South Asia via Indus Valley the Celts nearly made it as far as Tibet and contributed to the intangible heritage of the subcontinent.

There ought to be serious discussions about how the mysterious Indus script influence the interpretation of its date. Unfamiliar and isolated so far, the conclusions reached about them might change with the discovery of birch bark manuscript written in the Indus hieroglyphic script.[11] This evidence does not endorse the general notion about its Bronze Age antiquity. The original manuscript written in Indus script is in a museum in Afghanistan. Recent research conducted on the Kabul MS from a copy in Vienna Western Himalaya Archive (SNO5 1000, 7081) introduces alternative realities (3.8).[12] Birch bark manuscripts from

3.10 Kanishka Boddo coin, Gold stater, Wt.16.98 gm, Ahan Posh Tepe, Afghanistan. London: The British Museum

Gandhara in modern Afghanistan and Pakistan are peculiar to Kushana period synchronal to Roman Empire. Unfortunately, none of the objects presented here were discovered under controlled archaeological conditions. Birch bark manuscripts identified as Buddhist are written in Kharosti, which like Brahmi is adapted from Aramaic. In the Afghan Rabatak Inscription the Greco-Tocharian 'King of kings, Kanishka the Kushana, son of god (devaputra)' claims to have introduced 'Aryan' language in the region. Known to Chinese as Yüehchih (Moon Tribe) Kushana ushered Cultural Revolution in South Asia. Kanishka ruled an empire extending from Turfan in the Tarim Basin to Pataliputra on the Gangetic plain. The Oxus Gonur objects and the birch bark Kabul MS when seen together with the Indus seals indicate that they not only coexist but corroborate their universal genetics peculiar to Greco-Roman culture.

In scientific research on genetics India was a new starting point for migration. It brings us back to Ptolemy's knowledge of the world stretching from the Mediterranean to the Indian Ocean with China at the farthest end of the world. During this unprecedented transnational interaction, from Roman Britain to Han China, the 'big cat' of the Sundarbans widens our perspective on the cult of rejuvenation. Cult of the tiger from Roman Britain to the BMAC (Bactria Margiana Archaeological

Complex) and from Indus Valley to Han China surged forward suddenly at a time when world awoke to a new hope in eternal life. Tiger is not native to any of these regions. At the fulcrum is the royal Bengal tiger in the Bay of Bengal. The Sundarbans is home to cult of tiger god and Bonabibi, mistress of the tiger king. The hapless villagers of the Sundarbans the Beautiful Forest have surrendered to Bonabibi, the forest goddess. They have also devised ways to appease Dakshin Raya, the tiger god. The folk epic comes from a much older oral tradition, about which we can only deduce from the Indus seals since we have no other evidence.

Religious belief on Bonabibi and Zenda Ghazi is swayed by legend of ancestors and history of the place. The sub-category of the fantastic myths is magic and supernatural events. Two major themes run through most Epic Fantasy. One is the great quest and the other is the struggle between opposing forces, struggle between good and evil, light and dark or order and chaos. At the center is the main character striving to defeat the opposing forces or at best achieve balance. The oral composition of Bonabibi Pala is comparatively short but has the usual set of conventions. It has heroes who embody cherished values, face conflict with those values and more importantly, wage battle with forces larger than themselves and beyond their control. Actions of Dhuke are significant because they affect at a deeper level. The oral narrative is an exciting story with strong characters that shores up hope and strengthen the will to live.

The other major theme 'Quest' reveals the civilization's values and meaning. Quests always show the way to something that is a spiritual or religious undertaking. The folk epic is essentially a story of survival against great odds. The theme of quest translates as a quest for survival that leads village dwellers to magical Bonabibi and Zenda Ghazi who protect them from overwhelming dangers. In the epic pattern a quest also includes helpers who may appear in human or animal form. They assist the hero with their knowledge and magical powers, without them he would never succeed. In the lived in epic of Bonabibi, the Muslim fakirs are the supernatural guides who accompany group of wood-cutters and honey gatherers to sing songs and recite incantations in order to tame tigers and render them powerless. In the tide and the tiger country where life is unpredictable the performance of Bonabibi Pala is empirical. Witnessing the epic ballad repeatedly reaffirms faith in life.

There are four aspects of the epic tradition, namely the oral, the literary, the pictorial and the performing. They have a shared cultural setting and have coexisted in a lively relationship of exchange and interaction for all these centuries. The folk epic of the Sundarbans finds expression in oral, pictorial and the performing arts. The bridge between oral and literary form is the illiterate bard seated on stage at each performance as a prop pretending to read out from a book! The remarkably rich and amazing ballad is embedded in the folk tradition and yet fulfills the general conditions that eventually make a folk tale an epic. The performers continually recreate the ballad for village audiences scattered in the Sundarbans and thus ensure the continuity of the oral epic tradition. The song of Tiger King and the myth of Bonabibi has thematic development leading to crisis and tension. Songs of devotion act as interlude or digressions and the row musicians play traditional instruments sitting opposite to the bard. In the living epic tradition human protogonist is a subtext, as it were, for the glorification of supreme divine beings. Dukhe remains diminutive beside Bonabibi and Dakshin Raya and his role is merely to magnify the mighty supernatural beings.

MUSLIM LEGEND: Tiger Deity / Sylvan Saint

In *Ray-Mangal* Krishnaram Das told the story of Gahzi and the tiger in 1686. This earliest available literature comes from hundreds of years of living and remembering and retelling from generation to generation. Towards the end of 1800 Abdur Rahim wrote *Bonabibi Johuranama* in Bengali, but followed the Arabic custom of writing back to front. Bonabibi Pala is essentially a Musalmani legend. A metrical version of the Bonabibi Pala in Musalmani Bengali was composed by Munshi Bayanaddin Saheb under the title *Bonabibi Zahuranama*. It was composed on the 12th Bhadra (month) of 1281 B.S at Sivadaha (circa 1874).[13] A revised edition was printed in Calcutta in 1327 B.S.[14] The latest version of the epic fits into an existing powerful oral tradition. However, Munshi Bayanaddin Saheb elevated the folk epic to a truly profound level and thus enhanced its beauty and meaning. An abstract of the legend derived from this revised edition was published by Sarat Chandra Mitra in early 20th century in the Journal of the Anthropological Society of Bombay and elsewhere.[15] The legend mentions —

> The Musalmani female saint Bonabibi.
> Bonabibi's brother the Musalmani Shah Jangali.
> The Musalmani saints Badakha Zenda Ghazi and Badakha Kalu Ghazi.
> The Hindu tiger god Dakshina Raya or Raya Mani.[16]

Oral epic is a living legend in contemporary India. Banabibi Pala conveys the cultural ethos and the explicit role of epic in Hindu religion. According to S. C. Mitra, Dakshina Raya was the relative and commander-in-chief of Mukuta Raya, Raja of Brahmannagara in the district of Jessore now in Bangladesh. He was therefore entrusted with the administration of the Sundarabns, the southern part of the kingdom. For this reason Dakshina Raya was otherwise called the Bhatuvara or "The Lord of the 18 tides" (Bhatis)[17] According to other versions Bonabibi willingly shared part of the jungle with Dakshina Raya who ruled supreme in the area allotted to him. As regards the forest goddess Bonabibi and her brother Shah Jangali, it is said that they were born to Ibrahim in Mecca and were transported by air to Sundrabans to protect the believers. They came to live in the Bhati-desa to protect poor farmers and low caste fishermen, wood cutters and honey gatherers oppressed by Dakshina Raya. Ultimately defeated in battle Dakshina Raya was obliged to surrender as a the vassal of Bonabibi.[18] Inexplicably connected to Bonabibi is the legend of Zenda Ghazi who is declared the son of Shah Sekandar Badshah. But it is impossible to say who this Sekandar Badshah or Emperor Sekandar was. No relationship between Zenda Ghazi and Kalu Ghazi is mentioned in the legend in which Zenda Ghazi has 14,000 tigers as his guards. S.C. Mitra surmises that Kalu Ghazi is Zenda Ghazi's brother. Folk cult combines elements of myth as well as ritual. Zenda Ghazi seated under a golden canopy is described to be vermilion in complexion. By his side Kalu fanned Zenda Ghazi with a fan made of peacock feather and lotus-leaf.

For the purpose of preserving the past Sundarban's folk epic has been collected from various sources. It is from the revised edition published in Calcutta in 1327 B.S. that the abstract of this legend was published by S.C. Mitra:[19] Sarat Chandra Mitra's writing on "A Musalmani Legend about the Sylvan Saint Bonabibi and the Tiger-deity Dakshina Raya" provides translation of Munshi Bayanaddin Saheb's "Bono Bibi Zahuranama" in an abbreviated form.[20] Bano Bibi is a female saint of Musalmans assimilated in the Hindu pantheon as a goddess of Lower Bengal.[21] Bonabibi, like other Mahomedan saints such as Pir Gorachand, Manik Pir and Ola Bibi, is revered and worshipped by the native Musalmans living in the 24-Parganas and in other parts of Lower Bengal.[22] Her devotees erect dargas or small mounds of earth in her honor and sacrifice fowl thereupon in fulfillment of vows made by them.[23] Mitra has also published a paper "On Some Curious Cults of Southern and Western Bengal" including a folk-song invoking "Mother goddess" and "Dame of the Forest" sung by fakirs accompanying parties of wood-cutters in the Sundarban.[24] It appears from the legend recounted in Mitra's paper published below, that this female saint Bonabibi also "keeps watch and ward over the forest at the command of Allaah," and that she is "The mother or protector of destitute persons and all creatures living in the forests of 18 divisions of Lower Bengal. She also relieves the sorrows and miseries of all those who invoke her assistance by calling her as their mother." [25] On the whole Bonabibi Pala raises compelling new issues for the study of epic, as we examine concerns such as national identity, gender, pedagogy, ecology and conservation.

TRANSLATION BY MITRA : Chanted Narrative / Katha-Vachana Tradition

Boatman named Dhonai lived in a town called Kalinga. He made preparations to undertake an expedition to the forest for the purpose of collecting honey and wax. He desired to take with him as his companion a young nephew named Dukhe who lived with his widowed mother. With this objective in view, Dhonai went to Dukhe's house and broached to him the subject that was uppermost in his mind. Thereupon Dukhe enquired: "Uncle Dhona! Where will you go to? The latter replied: "O Dukhe! I have made up my mind to go on an expedition to the forest for gathering honey and wax. I want to take you with me as my companion. I have, therefore, come to you to obtain your assent to my proposal. You will have only to sit in the boat, beat a kettle-drum, and thus spend your time happily."

Dukhe rejoined: "I shall always stay in the boat and shall never go into the forest."

Dukhe's mother, who was present while the foregoing conversation was proceeding, said to Dhonai: "Dukhe is a widow's only son. He is the sole hope and stay of my life. How shall I send him away with you?"
Hearing these words, Dhonai gave in to Dukhe's mother and, addressing her, said: "Don't be anxious."
Thereafter Dhonai and Dukhe went away.
Seeing both of them leave, Dukhe's mother cried out, saying:
"Mother Bonabibi! Where art thou?
Dukhe, who is the (only) son of an unfortunate woman (like myself), is going on an expedition for gathering honey and wax. Thou art the mother of the destitute (and) the destroyer of (all) dangers. You should protect my (son) Dukhe (from all dangers). O mother! I have delivered him to thy care (literally, placed him at thy feet). O Bonabibi! (you) should protect (my) son (from all dangers) wherever he may be.

Having reached home, Dhonai got ready seven boats and filled them with provisions sufficient to last the whole period of the expedition. Then, accompanied by Dukhe and the boats' crew, he set sail from Kalinga after invoking the aid of Raya Mani (Dakshin Raya, the Tiger god).

Having rowed past various places, Dhonai and his party arrived at a place called Natakhali where they spent the whole night singing and dancing to the accompaniment of Dukhe playing on the kettle-drum. When the day dawned, Dhonai told his servants and retainers:

"Let us go into the forest in search of honey and wax."
At the same time, he ordered Dukhe to stay in the boat and play on the kettle-drum while he and his men were away in the forest. Then, devoutly invoking the aid of Dakshin Raya (or Dakshina Raya or Raya Mani), Dhonai and his retainers landed from the boats and went inside the forest for the purpose of gathering honey.

Dhonai and his men wandered through the forest all day long in search of honey, but could not find a single honeycomb, as Raya Mani had become displeased with him and miraculously concealed all the honeycombs in the forest. After this wild-goose chase, they got depressed in spirit and returned to their boats in the evening.

Dhonai lay down in the boat without taking any food or drink and began to complain of his hard lot. He regretted all the expense and the money that had been uselessly invested. He said to himself: "Why has the Dakshin Raya become displeased with me?"

While Dhonai lay asleep in this disturbed state of mind, he dreamt a dream, in the small hours of the morning, wherein he saw that the deity Raya Mani had come to him and was sitting near his head. In this vision, he heard the deity enquiring of him as to whither he would go with his boats. He replied to the godling as follows:

"O Raya Mani (or Dakshin Raya)! I submit (the following words) for your kind consideration (at your feet). I have come with the boats for gathering honey and wax.
Accept (my) worship (and) offerings (sacrifices) of incense.
Give me seven boatloads of wax and honey.
Having invoked your aid (literally, having thought of you),
I have come with the boats. I know of no other (patron-deity) except you. Grant (my) prayers [literally, heed (my) words] by giving (me) wax and honey. Otherwise (I) shall die [literally, give up (my) life] before you.

Hearing these words, Raya Mani felt compassion for Dhonai and said: I do not want any other offering except the sacrifice of the widow's son Dukhe. If you offer him to me, I shall give you a whole marketful of honey which I have kept reserved for you in the forest of Madhukhali. After offering Dukhe to me, you may load your seven boats with wax and honey and go away."

In reply, Dhonai said: How can I offer you Dukhe as he is the only son of a widowed mother ? I shall propitiate you with the offering of sheep and buffaloes. (Do be good enough to) grant Dukhe, who is the treasure of a destitute widow, as alms-offering to me.

By way of rejoinder, the godling Raya Mani (or Dakshina Raya) said: * (The words used in the printed version of this legend are missing.)
As Raya Mani or Dakshina Raya took up his residence in that forest, (Dhonai) worshipped him (placed at Raya's feet) with various offerings, (namely) sugar, large sugar-wafers, soft sweetmeats (called sandesh), various other kinds (of sweets), incense and perfumes. (In this way) the boatman Dhonai worshipped (the deity) Raya Mani on a Saturday.

After the puja (ritual worship) was over, Dhonai gathered one honeycomb and said to himself: "I am offering Dukhe to you. Now be good enough to grant me permission to load my seven boats with wax and honey to overflowing."

In response to Dhonai's prayer, the godling Dakshina Raya, by means of a voice from the sky, permitted him to gather wax and honey from the forest. Having received this permission, Dhonai, accompanied by his men, went into the forest to collect wax and honey while Dukhe stayed back in the boat and played on a kettle-drum.

By the grace of Dakshina Raya, Dhonai gathered seven boatloads of wax and honey and, then, set sail for Kedokhali (or Kendokhali). Having arrived there, he moored his boats on a sandbank and spent the night in sound sleep.

The next morning Dhonai ordered Dukhe to go into the forest for the purpose of cutting wood for fuel. But Dukhe refused saying that one of the boatmen should be sent for the purpose. Thereupon Dhonai got angry and, with the assistance of his men threw Dukhe overboard. Thereafter he set sail homewards and arrived at his native village with his boats.

As soon as Dukhe had been thrown from the boat on to the sandbank, Dakshina Raya (or Raya Mani), assuming the form of a gigantic tiger appeared. His mouth extended from the sky to the nether regions, his teeth gnashing with fury were as big as the rice-husking pedal and his breath was blowing through his nostrils like a violent tempest. With his eyes brighter than the sun and the moon, emitting flames of fire like so many lightning flashes, Dakshina Raya appeared before him. Seeing this terrible beast Dukhe's limbs began to quake with fear. Thinking that his last moments had arrived he wept bitterly and cried out:

"O mother Bonabibi! Come, come and save me from death at the hands of the tiger-demon Dakshina Raya. You promised me before that you would do this for me." Saying this, he became unconscious and fell down upon the ground.

Hearing Dukhe's piteous cries for help, the Sylvan Saint Bonabibi appeared before him and, finding him lying insensible on the ground, pronounced the Powerful Name (of the Almighty) (and) breathed upon Dukhe's body. Upon this action Dukhe recovered his consciousness, rose and sat up (upon the ground).

Thereafter, the female saint, who was the "mother of the 18 divisions", took him up on to her lap, and, seating herself on the sandbank at Kedokhali, said to him: "My dearest child! Do not fear anyone. Nobody within the 18 divisions, over which I have jurisdiction, will dare kill you." Saying this, she summoned her brother Jangali to come to her. Hearing her summons, Jangali, who lived within the 18 divisions over which she had jurisdiction, armed with a club arrived at a place where his sister Bonabibi was seated with Dukhe on her lap. Addressing her brother, she said: "Brother! Why are you staring at me? This tiger has come to kill and eat Dukhe. Do be good enough to expel this beast."

Hearing her command, Jangali, who was the son of Ibrahim, took up the club in his hands and dealt the tiger godling Dakshina Raya several blows on the head which split it open into two pieces. Getting frightened at this savage attack and fearing that he would lose his life at Jangali's hands; he turned tail and fled as fast as his legs could carry him. His assailant also gave chase and ran after him till both of them arrived at Kumarkhali.

Being very much frightened, Dakshina Raya began to quake in all his limbs and made his appearance before Zenda Ghazi. By this side Badakha Ghazi Kalu, with the palms of his hands joined together, was also seated.

Seven tigers stood in front of him.

Zenda Ghazi seated beneath a golden canopy is the son of Shah Sekandar Badshah who is a favourite of God.

The complexion of his body was like the colour of vermilion or unalloyed gold.

He was like an image made of light and emitted radiance like the moon's rays.

Zenda Ghazi, who gave a tent, which extended over the whole universe also gave countless treasures consisting of diamonds and various other gems.

He was seated like a beautiful image. He had fourteen thousand tigers as his guards.

While Kalu was fanning Zenda Ghazi with a fan made of peacock's feathers and lotus leaves, Dakshina Raya appeared before him. After arriving there, Dakshina Raya fell down senseless at Zenda Ghazi's feet. Seeing his wounds the Ghazi uttered the Powerful Name of the Almighty and lightly rubbed his body with the palms of his hands, whereupon the tiger deity's wounds healed up at the command of God, and his head became flat and extended (smooth) like a piece of plank.

Thereafter the Ghazi enquired of Dakshina Raya about the person who had insulted and injured him thus. On this, the godling informed of the circumstances under which the boatman Dhonai had offered his nephew Dukhe as sacrifice and as a reward had obtained seven boatloads of wax and honey. When he had gone to eat Dukhe in the form of a tiger the would be victim's piteous cries for help had brought the Sylvan Saint Bana Bibi to rescue and at the Saint's command, her brother Shah Jangali had broken his head and chased him with a view to kill him.

The tiger god further told the Ghazi: "I fear that Jangali would kill me. I have therefore come to you for protection. Do be good enough to save me from death at Jangali's hands."

The Ghazi replied: "Dakshina Raya! Do not fear. I shall certainly save you from death at Jangali's hands." Hearing these words, Raya Mani was comforted.

The words used in the printed version of this legend are:

At this time, Bonabibi's brother Jangali arrived there. Zenda Ghazi enquired of him as to why he had come thither. The former replied that he had been sent by his sister Bonabibi to arrest Dakshina Raya and take him to her.

At first, the tiger god refused to accompany Jangali to Bonabibi's place of residence. But the messenger said that in case of non-compliance with her order Dakshina Raya's punishment would be increased.

Hearing this threat, Dakshina Raya consented to go to Bonabibi on condition that the Ghazi should accompany him thither. Zenda Ghazi having agreed to do so, all the three set out for the place where the female Saint was staying with Dukhe.
When they arrived before Bonabibi, Dakshina Raya made salaam to her.

Then, addressing Bonabibi, Zenda Ghazi said:

"O benevolent mother ! Hear what I have to say. Mother! I crave this boon from your honoured self. Do away with your anger against Dakshina Raya. It is for this purpose that I have come to your honoured self."

Hearing these words, Bona Bibl felt compassion for Dakshina Raya, and said:

"I am the mother of all (who live) in the 18 divisions (of Lower Bengal). Whoever invokes me as (his) mother, (all) his sorrows (and) miseries are removed. Do not, under any circumstances, show any ill-feeling whatever to whomsoever, having fallen into a difficulty, will call (me) as (his) mother."

Hearing these words, Dakshina Raya replied:

"O mother! Hear what I am saying.
I solemnly vow thrice (before you) that whoever will come to the forest (and) invoke (you) as (his) mother, no harm whatever will be done to him by me."

Having received this solemn promise Bana Bibi was satisfied. Dakshina Raya and Zenda Ghazi departed from her presence.

The prologue and concluding part are missing in the printed version published by S. C. Mitra who ended by saying: With the remaining portion of the legend, I am not concerned. However he sets out elaborate patterns of relationships and origins of various personages in the folk epic.

FOLK EPIC IN INDIA: Folklore / Environment Conservation

In the theatrical rendering of Bonabibi Pala, the lengthy narrative is split into episodes and scenes according to epic traditions. Performers have developed a variety of strategies to engage their audience through skillful manipulation of music, meter and textual patterns that draws from wide variety of options. Songs perform critical structural role and manipulate mood. The prose narration and comments are linked to poetic chants. The performing artist, who is frequently an illiterate, is responsible for the aesthetic criteria of oral epic. These skilled professionals recreate the epic of Bonabibi to the village audience as a magical act that reinforce the protection of powerful deities. Recitation of myths and religious observances is a form of offering to deities. Hence, performing arts believed to be a gift of gods find a place in the temples or in temporary shrine installed for the purpose. Or a simple stage is transformed into a shrine and the performance concludes with ritual offerings in a traditional manner. Even in votive terracotta a sacred edifice provides the background for glorification.

Several societies commit to memory what they value most. There are variety of itinerant performers, who for centuries have preserved recollection by means of songs and endless retelling. Informal performances in various Indian languages take many forms, such as recitation, story-telling, ballad singing, puppetry, pageants, processions and even comedy. Folk epics in contemporary Bengal are spread by the artist-bards from the countryside who travel abroad with their painted narrative scrolls (patachitra). As part of a living tradition artist-bards maintain the oral epic tradition and help to strengthen cultural roots. The role of epic has been twofold, to commit to memory in poetic form the fundamental beliefs of a people and preserve their tradition. The epic stories over the time have become part of religious faith. Myths amplify traditional customs and religious beliefs. From ancient times narrative song is popular medium for storytelling. Narrative folk songs preserve and validate religious beliefs and rituals. Naturally each cult has singular songs composed for a specific deity to be recited for a particular reason on a particular occasion. For instance cult of Bonabibi entwined with cult of tiger god Dakshina Raya differs from the snake goddess Manasa cult.

In the Sundarbans agreement between humans and supernatural non-humans is advantageous. Reverence accorded to the tiger and the tree goddess was a way to gain trouble free life. In this conservationists' dreamland, outsiders consider the royal tiger elixer of life and a means to gain wealth. The tiger is ruthlessly hunted for its body parts. In contrast, Bonabibi and Gazi Pir offer protecting to both tiger and humans. Theatrical performance in community worship is sympathetic magic for survival of both. It may be said that seeking the help of Bonabibi and at the same time overcome the anxiety by propitiating the tiger demon continually upholds the Bonabibi Pala. The cult of heroes is a subtext, as it were, for the development of epic traditions that deal with larger questions of life and death. Bonabibi sharing the platform with Shah Jangoli and Gazi Pir is at the core of hero worship. Power of the divine female equally shared by the Pir can be a subject of interest. But it is the unambiguity of power that is intriguing. However, in mythology the goddess commands supremacy and without fail slays evil forces and offers protection. Bonabibi is goddess Ban Durga and this religious belief has been reinforced for centuries through rituals performed throughout the sub-continent.

Oral folk epic in India is rooted in geographically circumscribed circumstances and socio-religious contexts.[26] Dhukhe the sorrowful confined within these parameters finds salvation in the timeless forest. In the earliest cultic patronages Buddha (Gk. BODDO) identified with the lion is modeled on Hellenistic Apollo (3.9).[27] Introduced at the same time, reverence accorded to the tiger goddess and Gajalakshmi lustrated by elephants is a living tradition in India. At the centre of the ever widening circle of proliferating pantheon is the tree goddess with animal escorts. Today goddess riding the tiger king is worshiped as Bonabibi, Ban Durga and Bhavani meaning giver of life. It signifies the power of nature as the source of creative energy. Ultimately the global expansion of the tiger cult indicate the coming together of diverse groups of people. Here lies the pattern of development for the medieval cult of Gazi Pir and Bonabibi with its lateral link to prehistoric cult of the goddess and the tiger in the Indus Valley. With ever expanding global audience, the cult and the oral epic need not exhaust itself in its circumscribed area.

REFERENCES

1. In this difficult terrain where the earth literally slides from beneath one's feet the Royal Bengal Tiger roams and its ferocity is reputedly increased due to the saline water that it drinks!
2. The Sunderbans are a UNESCO World Heritage site. The ecosystem of Sundarbans is listed separately in the UNESCO world heritage as the Sundarban National Park and the Sundarban in east and west.
3. The mangrove forests of Sundarbans in the Gangetic delta are home to various cults. On the lap of River Ganga worshipped as a goddess resides Kapil Muni , an incarnation of Vishnu interwoven with the legend of Shiber Kumir, the crocodile of Lord Shiva from whose locks Ganga descended to redeem the souls of the thousand sons of King Sagara languishing in the underworld after they were burnt to ashes by Kapil Muni.
4. Gupta, G. K. Bon bibi in Sunderbans. The Tribune. Saturday, 2006 July 8.
5. Sir Edward's reference to the cult of Bonabibi in paragraph 524 mentioned by S. C. Mitra is to be found in Ethnography of Bengal, Gait's Report on the Bengal Census of 1901, that gives further information is given about Zend.i or Zindah Ghazi.
6. The Journal of the Asiatic Society of Bengal, Vol. LXXII (Part III) for 1903: 48.
7. Mitra, S.C. Cure Charm No. III In: The Journal and Proceedings of the Asiatic Society of Bengal (N. S.), Vol. XI,

1915: 225-226. Vide Mitra's article, A Musalmani Legend. In: The Journal of the Anthropological Society of Bombay, 171-172.

8. Pittman, Holly. *Art of the Bronze Age: Southeastern Iran, Western Central Asia, and the Indus Valley*. New York: The Metropolitan Museum of Art, 1984:50-51.

9. Ibid. 1984:70. Antelope that looks like goat is Caprid (Plural: Capridae).

10. Nagy, Gregory, *Homeric Questions*. York-Melbourne: Cambridge University Press, 1996: 44. Nagy quotes Stuart Blackburn in his introduction to *Oral Epics in India* (1989:27): "Tracing a narrative pattern that moves from a local hero toward a wider, more pan Indian identity for the hero/god [Blackburn] concludes that this change is a response to differing social groups and context encountered as an epic spread geographically."

11. John Newberry. Indus script monographs. Volumes 1-7, 1980: 10-20. Starting with Cunningham in 1877, some early scholars such as G.R. Hunter, S. R. Rao, F. Raymond Allchin, John Newberry, Iravatham Mahadevan and Krishna Rao thought that the system was the archetype of the Brahmi script. This is perfectly logical if we remove the inexplicable intervening gap between the two innovative scripts.

12. http://www.indoeurohome.com/LucyZuberbuehlerindusscriptmss2009.pdf A comparison of the manuscript with the Indus script. Lucy Zuberbuhler, 2009 Bachelor thesis, University of Bern, Institute Of Linguistics.

13. Blackburn. *Oral Epics in India*, 1989. Introduction, pp.1-11. Patterns and Development for Indian Oral Epic Tradition, pp. 33-54.

14. The Kanishka stater (c.78 AD) was found in a relic deposit at Ahan Posh Tepe (Ahan Posh - Persian: Iron covered place) near the Afghanistan city of Jellalabad. Coins of the Kushana king Kanishka (c.78-103 AD) together with a gold coin of the Roman emperor Trajan and empress Sabina minted in 128-137 AD was found in a gold amulet inset with garnet. The Kanishka gold stater depicting Hellenistic sun god Helios is inscribed BODDO in Greek.

15. In 2009 we are in 1416 B.S. (Bengali Calendar), which dates the first known printing of the folk epic to 1874. Sivadahais possibly Sealdha in Kolkata. Calcutta is now renamed Kolkata.
16. That is nearly 100 years ago.
17. More recently Amitav Ghosh refers to the cult of Bonabibi in *The Hungry Tide*, 2005.
18. An illustration of the image of this deity has been published in The Journal of the Anthropological Society of Bombay, Vol. III, p. 105.
19. S. C. Mitra, "Cult of Dakshina Raya in Sunthern Bengal", The Hindustan Review (Calcutta), January 1923, pp. 167-171.
20. Ibid.
21. Printed and published by Afzaddin Ahmmad from No. 337-2, Upper Chitpur Road, Calcutta. The year 1327 B.S is 1920. It is further edited for present purpose.
22. http://www.archive.org/stream/journalofthedepa033455mbp/journalofthedepa033455mbp_djvu.txt/22.9.09
23. Sarat Chandra Mitra, "On Some Curious Cults of Southern and Western Bengal", The Journal of the Anthropological Society of Bombay, Vol. XI, pp. 438-454. Two folk-songs invoking "Mother-goddess" and the "Dame of the Forest" (Bano-Bibi or Bona-Bibi) of the Sundarbans sung by fakirs who accompany wood-cutters going into the forest are mentioned by S. C. Mitra. Information received by Mitra was from Maihammad Sahidullah, then Lecturer in Bengali, Dacca University. Ibid, pp. 440-441.
24. Bengali Hindus believe that the "Lady of the Flux" personified as Ola Bibi controlls cholera.
25. Fowls in honour of this saint were set free. These fowls are known as "Sana Bibi's fowls".
26. The Journal of the Anthropological Society of Bombay, Vol. XI, pp. 438-454. S. C. Mitra describes effigy of tiger god "Dakhin Rai" worshipped in Sunderbans and remarks about the taped cult songs he listening to in Kar's house.
27. This legend is widely current among the Musalmans of the Twenty-four Parganas. The proverb "Like unto uncle Dhona / Dhonai" refers to a cruel relative such as uncle Dhonai in the

legend. This saying is widely current among Musalmans living in the other districts of Lower Bengal and in other parts of this province.

BIBLIOGRAPHY

Abdur-Rahim: *Bon Bibir Karamoti orhat Bon Bibi Johuranama* (Bengali: The Miracles of Bon Bibi or Narrative of Bon Bibi Glory), circa 1800.

Ball, Warwick. *Rome in the East: The Transformation of an Empire,* London: Routledge, 2000.

Basu, Gopendrakrishna. *Banglar Laukik Debata* (Bengali), Kolkata: Dey's Publishing, 2008.29-34. Reprint1966.

Begley, V. and De Puma, R. D. *Rome and India: The ancient sea trade.* Madison: University of Wisconsin Press, 1991.

Bhasin-Malik, Kamaljit (Meeto), *In the Making: Identity Formation in South Asia.* Delhi: Three Essays-Collective, 2007.

Battacharyya, Asutosh. The Tiger-Cult and its literature in Lower Bengal. In: India. 27, No.1. (March 1947): 49-50.

Blackburn, Stuart H. et al., (Eds.) *Oral Epics in India.* Berkeley: University of California Press, 1989.

_____. *Folk Hero and Class Interests in Tamil Heroic Ballads.* Asian Folklore Studies, 37(1), 1978, 131– 49.

_____.*Death and Deification: Folk Cults in Hinduism.* Chicago: University of Chicago Press, 1997

Eaton, Richard Maxwell. *The Rise of Islam and the Bengal Frontier, 1204-1760.* Berkeley: University of California Press, 1993: 212-214.

Foley, John Miles. *The Myth of Manas: A Study in the Popular Hinduism of Medieval Bengal.* Berkeley and Los Angeles: University of California Press, 1990

_____. *Epic as genre: Oral Epics in India*, Berkeley and Los Angeles: University of California Press, 1989

G.B., *The Deer and the Tiger; A Study of Wildlife in India.* Chicago, Chicago University Press.

Ghosh, Amitav. *The Hungry Tide.* New Delhi: Harper-Collins Publishers India, 2005: 101-105, 354-360. 5th edition.

Harlan, Lindsey. *The Goddesses' Henchmen: Gender in Indian Hero Worship*. New York and Oxford: Oxford University Press, 2003.

Jalais, Annu. Bonbibi: Bridging Worlds. Indian Folklife, Serial No. 28, January 2008:6-8.

http://wiki.indianfolklore.org/images/7/7a/Ifl_28.pdf/ Recovered 2014 July 28.

http://www.youtube.com/watch?v=jx5QXLZ6el0/Recovered 2014 July 2 [Biswajit Halder]

Mitra, Sarat Chandra. Saint Bana-Bibi and the Tiger-deity Dakshina Raya. 1923

http://www.archive.org/stream/journalofthedepa033455mbp/journalofthedepa033455mbp_djvu.txt/Recovered2009Sept. 22.

_____. A Musalmani Legend *about the Sylvan Saint Bana-Bibi and the Tiger-deity Dakshina Raya*. In: The Journal of the Department of Letters, Vol. X, Calcutta University Press, 1923: 171-72.

http://www.archive.org/stream/journalofthedepa033455mbp/journalofthedepa033455mbp_djvu.txt/22.9.2009

http://archive.org/stream/anthropologicalp032852mbp/anthropologicalp032852mbp_djvu.txt/Recovered/Recovered 2014July 28.

_____. On Some Curious Cults of Southern and Western Bengal. In: The Journal of the Anthropological Society of Bombay, Vol. XI, NO. 7. pp. 438-454.

_____. "The Worship of the Sylvan Qddett. In: The Hindustan Review, Allahabad, March 1917: 180-186.

_____. Cult of Dakshina Raya in Southern Bengal. In: The Hindustan Review, Calcutta, January 1923: 167-171.

_____. The Cult of Dakshina Raya in Southern Bengal. In: The Journal of the Asiatic Society of Bengal. Vol. LXXII (Part III) 1903: 48.

_____. Exorcising venom of scorpion. In: The Journal and Proceedings of the Asiatic Society of Bengal (N. S.), Vol. XI, 1915: 225-226.

Niogi, Tushar. *Tiger Cult of the Sundarbans*. Calcutta, Anthropological Survey of India, 1996.

Niyogi, Tushar K. *Tiger Cult of the Sundarvans.* Delhi: Vedam Books, 1996

O'Malley, Gazetters of Bengal District, 1914:13.

Padel, Ruth. *Tigers in Red Weather.* London Little Brown, 2005.

Rissman P.C. The Organisation of Seal Production in the Harappan Civilization. In : Old Problems and New Perspectives in the Archaeology of South Asia. (ed.) J.M. Kenoyer. 1989 : 159-170. Madison, WI, Wisconsin Archaeological Reports.

Sumanta, Banerjee, *Logic in a Popular Form, Essays on Popular Religion in Bengal*, Calcutta Seagull, 2002.

Sunquist, Fiona and Sunquist, Mel. *Tiger Moon.* Chicago: Chicago University Press, 1988.

Thapar, Valmik. *Land of the Tiger: A Natural History of the Indian Subcontinent.* University of California Press.

———. *The Tiger's Destiny.* London: Kyle Cathie, 1992.

———. *The Secret Life.* London: Hamish Hamilton, 1989.

———. *The Portrait of a Predator.* London: Collins, 1986.

———. *The Tigers in the Wild.* New Delhi: Vikas, 1982.

Toovey Jr. (ed.) *Tigers of the Raj.* Gloucester: Alan Sutton, 1987.

Wilson, R. J. A. Piazza Armerina. In: Akiyama, Terakazu (Ed.) The Dictionary of Art. Vol. 24: Pandolfini to Pitti. Oxford, 1998.

Majumdar, Dr. R. C. *The Classical Accounts of India.* Calcutta. 1960 103–128; 170–172; 198, 234.

Uddin, Sufia Mendez. Bonbibi, Protectress of the Forest. In: John Renard (Ed.) *Tales of God's friends: Islamic hagiography in translation.* Berkeley: University of California Press. 2009: 301–10.

_____.Beyond National Borders and Religious Boundaries: Muslim and Hindu Veneration of Bonbibi. In: Mathew N. Schmalz and Peter Gottschalk (Ed.) *Engaging South Asian Religions: Boundaries, Appropriations, and Resistances.* New York: State University of New York Press. 2011: 61–82.

McCrindle, John W. *Ancient India As Described in Classical Literature.* Delhi: Munshiram Manoharlal Publishers, 1901: 201.

Schoff, Wilfred H. (1912). *The Periplus of the Erythraean Sea.* London: Longman, Green and Co, 1938: 47–48.

Marshall, John. *Mohenjo-Daro and the Indus Civilization.* London: Arthur Probsthain, 1931. 3 vols. (Ed.) B.L. Eichler et al. New Delhi: J. Jetley for Asian Educational Services, 1996. Reprint.

Possehl, Gregory (Ed.) *Harappan Civilization: A Contemporary Perspective.* Delhi: Oxford University Press & IBH Publishing, and A.I.I.S., 1982.